*It's Good
to Be a Little
Selfish*

MOTHERS

NEED

TIME-OUTS,

TOO

*It Actually
Makes You a
Better Mother*

Susan Callahan • Anne Nolen • Katrin Schumann

New York   Chicago   San Francisco   Lisbon   London   Madrid   Mexico City
Milan   New Delhi   San Juan   Seoul   Singapore   Sydney   Toronto

The McGraw·Hill Companies

Library of Congress Cataloging-in-Publication Data

Callahan, Susan.
 Mothers need time-outs, too : it's good to be a little selfish—it actually makes
you a better mother / Susan Callahan, Anne Nolen, and Katrin Schumann.
  p. cm.
 ISBN-13: 987-0-07-150807-0 (alk. paper).
 ISBN-10: 0-07-150807-4 (alk. paper)
  1. Mothers—Psychology—Miscellanea. 2. Mothers—Conduct of life—
Miscellanea. 3. Self-help techniques. 4. Relaxation. 5. Pleasure.
 I. Nolen, Anne. II. Schumann, Katrin. III. Title.

 HQ759.C256 2008
 646.70085'2—dc22   2007029387

1 2 3 4 5 6 7 8 9 10 11 12 13 14 15 16 17 18 19 20 21 FGR/FGR 0 9 8

ISBN 978-0-07-150807-0
MHID   0-07-150807-4

Interior design by Yellow House Studio

McGraw-Hill books are available at special quantity discounts to use as premiums and
sales promotions or for use in corporate training programs. To contact a representative,
please visit the Contact Us page at www.mhprofessional.com.

This book is printed on acid-free paper.

CONTENTS

ACKNOWLEDGMENTS

This book wouldn't exist if it weren't for the many women all over the world who shared their personal stories with us—we simply can't thank you enough. Your innate wisdom and willingness to be open taught us so much. Thanks to our agent, Stephanie Kip Rostan, the perfect advocate: clear-sighted, encouraging, and focused; and to our editor, Judith McCarthy, for her limitless energy and enthusiasm for this project. You have both been responsive and visionary, and we are so grateful.

Many thanks to the entire McGraw-Hill team especially Nancy Hall, our project editor, and Kenya Henderson, our publicist. Thanks to those who watered the seedling and helped it flourish: Marnie Cochran, who believed in our potential from the beginning and always left her door open for us; Betsy Cole, whose expertise as a life coach helped us dig deeper and made us push harder; Betsy Rosen, whose ideas and intellect were vital to the beginning of the project; and Jim Spencer, our steadfast Web guru who guided us smoothly through the maze of online marketing. Thanks to our five fabulous readers of the manuscript, whose feedback helped immeasurably: Diana Barrett, Elizabeth H. Cole, Dixie Coskie Freemont-Smith, Kristi Perry, and Ann Groccia. Also, many thanks to all who gave so generously of their advice and support: Alison Bailes, Tim Carroll, Mary Kaye Chryssicas, Meaghan Dowling, Carol Dunne, Dr. Richard Dupee, Jennifer Jordan, Kate Kellogg, Pam Knox, George Kostakos, Janet Lisle, Carol Mann, Liz Pryor, Jennifer Putnam, David Sabel, Linda and Peter Scull, Abby Seixas, Michelle Slatalla, Anne Wells, and Philip Van Munching.

Susan: Thank you to all the mothers in my life who have shown me the joys of bringing up children. My heart is full of gratitude that I have been able to share in this wonderful journey with you all! Thank you to my parents and sister who have always helped me anchor my thoughts and dreams. To Virginia Auciello and Jen Abbott who patiently listened and whose wisdom is beyond measure. To Kika, my saving grace, for helping me in every way imaginable so that I could be with the kids. And an enormous thank-you to Topher, my husband, for every single bike ride you went on with the kids so I could work on this book, and for continually letting me fill myself up with this project, year after year. I am so immensely grateful for your support, kind spirit, love of learning, and sense of humor.

Anne: To the countless people who traveled the journey of this book with me. Without your wisdom and advice, this book would not have been possible. You will all see yourselves in these pages—they're a culmination of your ideas. Through endless hours of navigating the roads of motherhood together, we have celebrated the good and processed the confusing. We now find ourselves surrounded by some amazing kids. My hope is that this will be a tool for *them* when they're raising kids of their own, to show them a snapshot of what we were thinking at this stage of the mothering game. This will be my payback to you.

Katrin: Thank you, Occu Schumann, the mother lion, who taught me that the deepest love is both tender and fierce. Also Sheila O'Marah, who has been my other mother for twenty years. Kevin—big-hearted, passionate, and just a little crazy— you make everything possible. Peter, Greta, and Svenja, you bring such lasting joy to a life-of-too-much-laundry! Thank you for being so patient, hilarious, and sweet; I am so proud of you. I'll always be grateful to Kathleen Buckstaff, who—with her infinite talent—is my touchstone, and Catherin Maynier, the sister I never had. Thanks to Francesca and Mark Nelson-Smith, so generous and inspiring, and my dear neighborhood friends: the best, most rockin' parents around, from whom I am always learning something new.

INTRODUCTION

From Never Being a Good-Enough Mother to Finding Happiness in Doing the Best You Can

O K, the truth is, we haven't solved every problem and we can't offer a cure-all. But with a combined thirty-five years of parenting a total of ten children, the three of us have discovered that being a little selfish (and trying to let go of the guilt) has helped us enjoy the mothering trip a whole lot more. And our families are better off for it—it's a win-win situation!

Our search for the answers to the perplexing question of how to be great mothers and still have full, calm, and satisfying lives independent of motherhood is what brought us together in the first place. We talked endlessly. We read loads of how-to books written by doctors, coaches, therapists, and celebrities. But we got tired of being told what to do by people with all the best intentions who often hadn't been in the trenches of motherhood themselves. Where were the stories from real women, warts and all? Well, they were few and far between. We yearned to hear solutions from regular mothers out there, so we could make up our *own* minds about how to achieve a more genuine happiness. So we started talking to other moms, too.

In the early years of our friendship, we focused on just making it through each day. But as our kids grew in inches and independence, everything started to shift. Off they went to school, and we were plagued by new, often bigger, and less clear-cut challenges: health scares, behavioral issues, out-of-control schedules, and a vague but very tangible sense of emptiness. Our lives sometimes seemed to lack achievable and satisfying *personal* goals. If ever we took any time for ourselves to read, enjoy a hobby, or take care of our own needs, we'd feel tons of guilt. So we kept talking.

Pulling back from the pack, we started to take a long, hard look at the lives we'd slipped into. The three of us couldn't have been more different, yet there we were on the very same high-speed train, racing through our hectic days. We considered our roles as mothers our most important calling in life; but no matter how hard we tried, we felt as though we were always coming up short. Boy did we ever need some grown-up time-outs just to catch our breath and regroup before charging ahead again!

Let's face it, as our kids were growing up, so were we. With those first gray hairs came a longer-term perspective on life that really rocked our worlds. Each of us started to wonder: What happened to my life? What happened to *me*, to my dreams? I thought I'd be so good at this, so why do I feel invisible and unsatisfied? The talking continued.

Susan was a hardworking businesswoman for fifteen years before stopping work cold turkey to raise her children. Anne is a busy doer who works in the city and tries to fit it all in. And Katrin is an artist and a writer, who flies by the seat of her pants and chafes at rules. Growing up, our experiences were all over the map: suburbs and city, United States and Europe, single mom and nuclear family, and mothers who worked full-time, worked part-time, or stayed at home. Yet here we were, three different women with three different approaches to life, all scratching our heads and asking the same question: *is it really OK to keep sacrificing ourselves for the sake of our families?*

Tips from the Trenches

We started gathering real-life stories from the trenches of motherhood. Soon we launched a blog and a newsletter and started running focus groups far and wide to get real solutions from the *real* experts. We dug deeper and deeper. We sent out global questionnaires and polls. We talked to mothers in libraries, supermarkets, schools, and hair salons from Ohio to California and from Maine to Montana.

What a mother lode we uncovered! We discovered that other women felt the same way we did—mothers across America, in Europe, and in Australia. It surprised us at first: whether a schoolteacher in Arizona, a lawyer in Texas, or a painter in France, modern mothers are fighting the very same battles. We all want the best for our children and our families; yet too often we lose ourselves along the way. Working mothers and stay-at-home mothers, young and old, organized and disorganized, all share a sense of being suffocated by the desire for perfection. Just talking about it was enough to start making everyone feel much better.

Through the intimate stories of these women, we discovered something huge: mothers need time-outs, too! Maybe they're cranky and just need a break. Maybe they're happily going full steam ahead and just deserve a break. Often they're fried from trying so hard, and they need to recharge their batteries to stay sane. Sometimes they need to press the Pause button so they can find themselves again. The bottom line is, time-outs are a good thing and being a little selfish isn't always bad.

Selfish moms—now that's a beautiful irony. Here we'd been trying so hard to be *selfless*, and suddenly we were proponents of being more *selfish*. But what really struck us was how strongly mothers identified with our message. No one really wanted to be called selfish (even when we mean it tongue-in-cheek), but every mother understood that by taking more time-outs, she could live a more balanced life.

We've spent the last few years talking to more than five hundred women, digging up the most recent research online and in journals, going to lectures and taking classes, and finding statistics and words of wisdom. We've immersed ourselves in Eastern philosophies, health studies, and parenting books, and we've listened to many stories from mothers like you, culling only the very best from all these resources.

Tools for Success

As the pervading sense of uncertainty and competitiveness began to lift from our shoulders, the three of us became convinced that we could help other mothers make peace with deliberate choices and balance the day-to-day chaos of motherhood with a sense of joy and reflection. We're passionate about our next mission: sharing this information with you so you can find your own way. We hope it will be as life-changing for you as it has been for us.

Our ongoing personal journeys show that any mother out there—whether type A or type Z, creative or linear, strict or easygoing, financially set or struggling—can use the same approach: being a little *selfish*, not more *selfless*, to find a more successful way of life.

We wrote this book for mothers who are searching for meaning, whether alone or with a partner, and can't seem to find their groove. It's for us businesswomen moms who put on our suits for work and leave the mess of home life behind, but can't always find the right balance for ourselves. It's for those of us who stay at home, yet feel as though we're drowning and so out of touch with what we really want for ourselves and our families that we no longer recognize ourselves. It's for the same-sex couples who fight the very same battles as conventional partners, losing themselves in the flurry of life. It's for the parents who've been struggling to start a family and find that having their dream child doesn't solve every problem.

With this book, you're about to begin a journey of self-discovery. Your willingness to open yourself up to scrutiny, to change habits, to ask for help, and to admit and even *relish* imperfection will help you regain control of your life. You'll learn to listen to your instincts again and to stop feeling guilty about never being quite good enough. You'll treat yourself with more compassion and become more patient with those around you. Everyone will be better off for it—trust us! We're everyday mothers whose lives are full of chores and children, house and work, love and war, and we finally feel pretty darn happy—and when we're not, we know it's OK. That's hugely empowering.

We're the first to admit that we're not celebrities or Ph.D.s, but we fight the good fight day in, day out, trying to find the right balance between being dedicated mothers and fulfilled women. Judging from the mothers we've talked to from all walks of life, we think we've uncovered a slew of smart solutions to help *you* achieve greater harmony in your family life. Many of these solutions involve slowing down, stepping back, gaining perspective, and giving yourself *time-outs* so you can live your life more deliberately and with a greater confidence.

You can decide for yourself which ideas might work for you, by reading about the trials of women just like you, as well as those who are the polar opposite. We won't tell you what to do; we'll show you what hundreds of other mothers have done, and you might choose to put these insights into practice in your own life—or not.

Our goal is to open your eyes to a new way of seeing yourself as a woman, friend, lover, and mother. It's going to be an empowering trip. Yes, sometimes it might be difficult. You'll probably face some truths about yourself and your relationships that you won't like much. But lay aside your feelings of remorse, blame, or inadequacy; put down the phone or the laundry. Read without guilt during your lunch hour, on the way to work, or at your kitchen table.

How to Get the Most from This Book

Although our first three chapters lay out the argument for embracing an alternative approach to motherhood, you don't have to read this book in order. Dip in and out; find yourself in any of its pages.

- Start a *Woman's Workbook*: pick up a small spiral-bound notebook from your local supermarket or get yourself a nice leather diary. This is for your personal scribbles and is for your eyes only.
- Take the journey with friends and lovers: having partners in crime will make the trip all the more fun! Get together and discuss ideas.

► Read our personal turning points: how the three of us continue to work at making the most of who we are might shed light on how you can accept your weaknesses while also capitalizing on your own strengths.

► Give the Tips from the Trenches at the end of each chapter a real go—not once or twice, but for an entire week at a time.

THE ATTITUDE SHIFT

From Trying to Be Perfect to Taking Time-Outs for Yourself

How often have you said, "It's crazy—life's so crazy! How did it get so exhausting? Why am I so busy?" We'll bet you say or hear that at least once a day, if not more often. Why has this complaint become the modern mother's mantra? Because we're consumed by the frenzy of *accomplishment*: the never-ending need to achieve, the push to always be the best, and the pressure not just to keep up, but to *exceed* expectations.

Who raised the bar so darn high? We live in a time when children play multiple sports every season of the year. Today's kindergarten curriculum used to be the first-grade curriculum. It takes hours to fill out forms so your kids can participate in school activities (and of course, you're supposed to have memorized their entire medical history). That special gift you got your child a few years ago? It's already been replaced by the high-definition version that parents and grandparents are waiting in long lines to get a hold of. Mothers are expected to look ten years younger than their real age: health clubs and diet centers are on every other corner. Homes are impeccably decorated, seemingly overnight, and they're expected to be picture-perfect at all times. The list goes on, and on, and on.

Conversations between us moms have started: We know it's all too much, but we don't know what to do about it. We're pulled along by the tide. Some of us say, "If you can't beat 'em, join 'em." But it doesn't have to be that way.

Trying to be perfect may be inevitable for people who are smart and ambitious and interested in the world and its good opinion. What is really hard, and really amazing, is giving up on being perfect and beginning the work of becoming yourself.
—Anna Quindlen, writer

It's high time to stop beating yourself up about your shortcomings and to start understanding the value of your efforts. Instead of limiting your life by suffering constant self-doubt or disappointment, you can free yourself to operate according to your own standards. Give yourself a break by taking some well-deserved time-outs. We hope to show you—through sharing the stories of hundreds of mothers just like you—that by being a little selfish, you can reclaim your right to make choices about how you run your life and the life of your family.

Come again—*selfish*? While most of the hundreds of women we spoke with cringed at the word *selfish*—because more than anything, they aspire to being more *selfless*—each and every one agreed that she felt better and did a better all-around job when her own needs were being met. "A high-quality life starts with a high-quality you," life coach Cheryl Richardson writes in *Take Time for Your Life*, "This means putting your self-care above anything else. . . . It's a challenging concept for most."

Mothers certainly mean well. But by sacrificing our own needs, we end up resentful and exhausted. It may sound crazy

FROM PROBLEM TO SOLUTION

Maureen, Mother of Two from Illinois

One afternoon Maureen sprinted from work to catch the early train home so she could watch her twelve-year-old play in an away basketball game. She ended up being late for the game, only to discover that her son had played in the first quarter and wouldn't be playing again. In the dingy stall of the girls' bathroom, she found herself on the verge of tears. "I felt like such a loser," Maureen said. "Like I just couldn't get anything right!" It was her son who turned things around for her. "Just come to the home games, Mom," he said, "if you can." She felt a huge sense of relief. If he wasn't even expecting her to do it all, why was *she*?

at first, but if women started paying more attention to themselves instead of doing everything for everyone else, everyone would be better off.

> *The greatest discovery of any generation is that human beings can alter their lives by altering the attitudes of their minds.*
> —Albert Schweitzer, scientist

Yes, it means taking quiet time *every day*. It means knowing yourself and determining your priorities. It even means sometimes putting yourself and your desires *before* those of the children. In some ways that seems radical; yet it's simple and ultimately, beneficial to all. If we've learned one thing from hours of conversation all over the country, it's this: when mothers muster up the courage to question the status quo, they begin to live well-rounded, calmer lives.

So we're here to grab you by the shoulders and say: Wake up! You're worth something! We're not talking about manicures and endless loafing around at the spa or in front of TV soap operas, or ignoring your children so you can advance your career or have more fun. It's not about whether you have time or money. It's about accepting that your efforts, goals, hopes, desires, fears, and opinions matter, and that by taking better care of yourself, you can take better care of those you love. Sophia, a mother of three from Rhode Island, couldn't quite get her head around this idea at first, but the more we all got talking, the more her eyes lit up. "My default mode is that I come last," she said. "I just thought that was the way it was supposed to be."

Facing Up to Reality

There *is* a magic bullet that can help you feel more balanced as a mother! Strip everything back to the basics to remind yourself about what your family's needs really are, and you'll realize that all the other stuff just doesn't matter that much—it's *optional*. This tiny adjustment in attitude can lead to changes so fundamental that the overall shift in how you feel—and as a consequence, how you live—is huge. A burden is lifted: the burden of living according to standards that are not achievable or sustainable—and not even yours.

We met so many women in our focus groups who suffer from trying to be everything to everyone. They often feel they *should* lead their lives in a certain way, doing all the *right* things. These *shoulds* become so overpowering that these women rarely take their own desires into account. Hannah is a single working mother who lives in California with her preteen daughter. "There's so much I have to make up for, being a divorced mom," she says. "All the time I feel like I should do this, I should do that. It's so draining!"

How Much of a Perfectionist Are *You*?

Having high standards is considered healthy behavior, right? So what is it about the standard of perfectionism that's so oppressive? Well, countless psychological studies point to links

SUSAN IS FORCED TO PARE IT DOWN

When I had my first baby, Charlie, I felt overwhelmed at times, but I also heard an inner voice saying I had to do it all, and do it all right: the nap schedule, walking the baby outside for fresh air, putting on a clean bib for each meal, doing a million mini-loads of laundry. The buck stopped with me.

After a few months, things were moving along pretty smoothly, and I went back to work. Eventually, baby number two, Cole, came along. Even though I was exhausted from being up in the night, I never went to bed until the house was all picked up. With the new baby, we set up a new schedule and devised a plan, and tick-tick-tick, I again went back to work full-time. Things were cruising along, or so I thought.

Then life happened. My main client was now in Europe. I was pregnant again. We hired live-in help. We bought a house. I juggled my work schedule so that I wouldn't miss the puppet show, the doctor appointments, or any client meetings. I still worked on strategic plans until midnight, cleared every dish, and filled out every school form on time. The voice in my head started shouting: don't stop, keep going, and keep doing, doing, doing. That's what moms do.

About a week after our third child, Hugh, was born, we unexpectedly had to let our sitter go and my husband,

Topher, broke his ankle. The kids missed the bus three times in a row, their school forms were late, we had no help, and unpacked moving boxes surrounded us.

I hit a wall—hard. My body was screaming at me that I couldn't do it all. I was so exhausted, but I simply had no choice. People were counting on me. My baby needed milk; my other kids had to be fed, clothed, and sent off to their new school; and even Topher was now dependent on me.

When I took a good, long look at our state of affairs, I realized this crazy situation was actually a gift. What were the most crucial things we needed for our survival? Food, sleep, clothes. I took my personal achievement bar and moved it way down.

That was the only thing that got me through that insane time. At that moment, I understood that I didn't need to do or have it all, and ironically, that "having it all" didn't even feel so good. Paring things down has always been hard for me, but I learned that if life doesn't go according to my own personal plan, sometimes I have to just go with the flow.

between perfectionism and dysfunction. "One of the most pernicious forms of self-generated stress stems from perfectionism," explains Dr. Jon Allen in a 2003 *Perspective* magazine article. A continuous cycle of striving, failure, and self-criticism creates stress, which pumps our blood full of hormones such as cortisol and epinephrine. Both have been proven to harm the immune system, making people more vulnerable to a variety of illnesses—from the flu to cancer. Perfectionists often want and expect others to be perfect, too, perpetuating the cycle and leading to disagreements, wrecked relationships, and even more stress. But Dr. Allen, a professor of psychiatry at Baylor College of Medicine, adds: "The good news is although perfectionism can be a relatively ingrained personality trait, it can be moderated over time."

> *The art of being wise is knowing what to overlook.*
> —William James, philosopher

Look at it this way: If you're setting your own standards and are happy fulfilling them, everything's all right. But if you feel that you're always failing, can't escape the craziness, and that it's all out of your hands, then you're probably aiming too high.

Do you see any of these tendencies in yourself?

- Whenever you make a mistake, you're very hard on yourself. You're always second-guessing your decisions.
- You find yourself getting angry when your family lets you down by making the house messy, not performing well, or not putting their best foot forward.
- Asking for help seems like a sign of weakness. You don't do it a lot.

- You don't like to think someone else is doing better (at anything) than you are. You often compare mental notes on other women's houses, marriages, and kids.
- Even though you don't want to, you find fault with your partner, kids, or friends more often than you think is normal.
- Other people's demands on you seem unreasonable or overwhelming, yet you don't want to disappoint by not living up to them.
- You believe that other mothers are "successful" without having to try so hard. They seem to make fewer mistakes and suffer less anxiety.
- When something unpredictable happens—and this seems to be the story of your life—you get really bent out of shape.
- Most of all, your everyday life does not meet your expectations, and you have a constant sense of failing at your most important calling: being a mother.

Surely almost every mother out there has felt some of these emotions at some point and hasn't liked the feeling. When this kind of behavior becomes chronic and starts to make you unhappy, *then* it's becoming a problem: maybe you need to give yourself a time-out and reassess!

Most of us have bought into the fantasy that we could have it all, if we wanted: a great job, a supportive and romantic

FROM PROBLEM TO SOLUTION

Carrie, Mother of Three from Massachusetts

Carrie loves living in the city, and her family of five shares a small house without many closets. She has to be incredibly organized with toys, books, art projects, clothes, and household supplies. "I like it neat anyway, but I really became such a nag about it all!" she explained. Instead of enjoying the way the house operated, she became obsessed and put out by even the smallest mess. Finally, she realized it was no fun being such a neat freak. "I figured it was better to find ways to tolerate some disorder, so the kids could be kids, and we could relax!"

husband, happy kids, a well-organized home, *and* a social life. Some can pull it all off with aplomb, and some buckle under the pressure. With supportive people around us—husbands, family, friends—it's easier to juggle all the different roles. Fathers of today have been asked to step it up and be much more available at home, both emotionally and physically, than they have in the past, and that certainly helps. But even with their goodwill, everyone's stretched to the limits.

On top of that, what about all the financial pressures that families face? It seems to be getting harder and harder to make ends meet—especially when you have super-high expectations. Our society has such an entrenched winner-take-all attitude. If you snooze, you lose. If you win, you're king! Everyone's working themselves to the bone trying to make ends meet, which only adds to the sense that taking a break and enjoying the *process* of life simply isn't possible. And when it comes to mothering, most of us just can't seem to help ourselves: for the sake of our children we want to be winners, and of course we want them to be winners, too.

We were surprised by how many mothers complained about the pressure of trying to be perfect, but felt incapable of stepping off the never-ending treadmill. But here's the deal: you can start shifting your attitude *right now*.

Getting Ourselves Out of This Pickle

How do we wrestle back a sense of control over a world that seems to be asking too much of us? Many of the mothers we talked to said they try to hang onto a sense of control by micromanaging, hoping this will help them feel better: "If only I get a grip on this and this and this, everything else will fall into place." But remember:

▶ **Trying to maintain control at all costs can turn you into a manic mother.** Have you ever been haunted all day long by the plates left on the kitchen counter or the shoes strewn around the hallway?

▶ **You become overly appearance conscious (i.e., your children, your house, yourself), getting caught up in the image your family projects to others.** When your child's socks don't match, no one is going to notice.

▶ **Because you become hyperfocused on details, you can miss the big picture.** Does it really matter how many shots your daughter got in during her basketball game, or is the fact that she happily high-fives her teammates when game time is over what really counts?

But wait, there's good news: the stress that perfectionism causes is entirely self-induced and therefore is optional! Tuning out or toning down the cacophony of voices and influences from the past and the present will help us set our own standards. Alice, mother of one from Connecticut, said she got so tired of the constant stress of trying to get her daughter to school on time that she decided it just wasn't going to be one of her priorities anymore. "Lilly got thirty-seven tardies this year, but I can't rush and I can't rush her," Alice said. "Our life is a work in progress!"

> *Freedom is not worth having if it does not include the freedom to make mistakes.*
> —Mahatma Gandhi, former leader of India

Today's mothers are among the first generation of women who were brought up fully believing they could become recognized leaders in all areas of life: industry, politics, business. According to the U.S. Bureau of Labor Statistics, between 1975 and 2005, labor force participation of mothers with children under eighteen rose from 47 to 71 percent. Anna from Ohio, stepmother of two teenagers and mother of a toddler, sees it this way: stay-at-home moms are desperately trying to prove they're as valuable as the CEO moms, while CEO moms want to prove they're just as nurturing as stay-at-home moms. How do both camps manage that? By running their families like businesses: relentless activity, ever-higher standards of success, zero downtime, and no mistakes tolerated.

FROM PROBLEM TO SOLUTION

Helen, Mother of Three from Virginia

Helen grew up in a home where the sheets were always pressed, her clothes were perfect, and she never missed a bath. When she first had kids, she drove herself crazy insisting that everything be done just the way her mother did it. Each day she engaged in power struggles with the kids and her husband. Then her own mother called her on it! "She complained that I was too controlling," Helen said. "She said it would end up hurting everyone." That was a real eye-opener. It turns out that life for her mother hadn't really been as perfect as it seemed, and she felt she'd sacrificed too much in her quest for control. Now Helen gives herself permission to skip some routines every now and then. And it's working: she's not as stressed, and everyone's fighting less.

Regardless of how exactly you spend your days, the following is indisputable:

- ▶ Ambitious women want results, whether in the home or in the office.
- ▶ It's hard to tell if you're doing a good job parenting.
- ▶ Often, your female role models are either outdated or illusory.

FROM PROBLEM TO SOLUTION

Carolyn, Mother of Two from Arizona

When her neighbor was moving, Carolyn, who used to be a professional chef, threw a luncheon for her: It would be the perfect send-off. She shopped until she dropped. The night before, Carolyn stayed up late printing photos for the gift bags. She got up early to get flowers from the farmer's market. "I was already feeling a bit overwhelmed," she admitted, "before anyone had even arrived at my house!" Then she realized the oven had never cranked up to the right temperature. The soufflé would be a total flop, and she hadn't even finished the gift bags yet! In a panic, she ended up ordering pizza and forgetting about the gifts altogether. "You know, I think I was actually *more* relaxed, because I just totally gave up," she said.

Some of our own mothers were prototypical "perfect moms," and we struggle trying to live up to those standards, even if our lifestyles are radically different. Or if our own mothers were neglectful, we're determined to make up for it by being the model mother we never had.

Consider this:

- ► Enjoying the fruits of your labors isn't about other people patting you on the back or looking at you with admiration. If *you* feel good about your efforts, that is good enough.
- ► Are your kids happy? Do they fall asleep at night tuckered-out and well-fed? Do they let you know they love you? In and of itself, that tells you you're doing all right.
- ► Role models are useful as reference points, but defining your own parenting style is the biggest favor you can do for yourself.

When Expectation and Reality Don't Quite Gel

In a perfect world, motherhood would be more predictable. We've spoken online and in person with so many bright, energetic women who began the motherhood journey full of zeal and goodwill, only to lose steam along the way when their standards weren't being met.

Often these ideals about perfect parenting are heightened at traditional occasions such as birthdays, Christmas, Hanukkah, Valentine's Day, Easter, Thanksgiving, and Halloween. Kids' birthday parties used to be simple affairs; now they're full-blown carnivals. The development of a whole industry geared toward kids' parties is an entirely modern phenomenon. And who invented the idea that the birthday child gives presents to the kids attending the party?

> *When you look at yourself from a universal standpoint, something inside always reminds or informs you that there are bigger and better things to worry about.*
> —Albert Einstein, scientist

Now here's a real Pandora's box: family dinners. Experts and mothers have a lot to say on that topic. Rita from Texas, mother of three boys, said family dinners were her Achilles' heel. "I know I should have them more often," she said, "but I just can't!" The president of the National Center on Addiction and Substance Abuse at Columbia University, Joseph A. Califano, Jr., reports, "Intensive research and teen surveys have consistently revealed that the more often children eat dinner with their parents, the less likely they are to smoke, drink, and use illegal drugs." Does that mean Rita doesn't care that she's potentially exposing her boys to risks? Of course not: Billie has hockey at 6:00 P.M., Taylor needs to be at play practice at

6:30 P.M., and Henry has piano at 7:00 P.M. Is Rita doomed to failure as a mother?

The fact is, you may know what the ideal scenario is, yet still be unable to provide it. What can you do about this? First, identify the problem, then set a small, achievable goal. Rita, for instance, decided never to schedule any activities for Sunday night, their *one* family dinner night now that's sacred to them.

Usually, when you step back and take a good, long look at these kinds of pressures, you realize that there's a pretty simple lesson in all this: if you can settle on some compromises, you can achieve a better balance. Mothers in our focus groups have suggested some ways to adjust your own comfort level:

▶ **Choose your priorities.** You can cut down on your children's activities to free up time for other things or for nothing. Afraid your child will lose out? Well, life's full of choices, and your child will learn that it's OK not to do everything all at the same time.

▶ **Focus on the real reason.** What's an event like a birthday party or a family dinner really about? It's about celebrating togetherness and having fun, not about proving how much effort you put into it. If the event is especially for kids, remember what matters to them: it's not the perfect decorations, but the fun with their friends.

▶ **Be realistic.** If you can't pull off the spectacular family Christmas every year, switch off with other family members.

If dinner together seven nights a week is just too much, try for three.

▶ **Be more flexible.** Figure out a different way to bond or celebrate that works for your family. You don't have to be the same as everyone else.

> *Sometimes we need to just do the best we can*
> *and then trust in an unfolding we can't design or ordain.*
> —Sharon Salzberg, spiritual teacher

FROM PROBLEM TO SOLUTION

Michelle, Mother of Four from Colorado

The morning of her third grader's first day at school, Michelle was handed a thick pamphlet. Twenty-five pages of requests for volunteers: there was chess club, softball, the school play, the math team, the science fair, and driving for field trips. Her heart sank. Even though Michelle works only part-time so she can participate in just this sort of thing, she immediately felt snowed under. Was she going to have *any* sort of a life of her own? "I felt so bad, like my kids would notice all the other moms helping out more than me," Michelle said. "But then I resorted to my old saying: 'We do things the way *our* family does them.' That quelled the panic."

You have high expectations of yourself, sure, but what about when *others*, too, have high expectations of you? Maybe your kid's school is always looking for volunteers, and whether you work or stay at home, you just can't fit it all in. Maybe your husband wants beautiful dinners every night or folded laundry at the ready. Does your boss ask you for extra work all the time, forgetting you've got a whole separate world of responsibilities to deal with once you get home? And what about your kids? They want something too—your time and attention.

Lower That Bar, Girl, You Can't Jump That High!

It goes without saying that women have to work hard at being great mothers. It's a huge and vitally important responsibility. But surely it's not to anyone's advantage if we work like dogs. A 1999 University of Texas study states: "There is evidence that given similar levels of talent, skill, or intellect, perfectionists perform less successfully than nonperfectionists." Ouch! So we're actually *hurting* ourselves and our families by insisting that everything be "right" and "perfect." Let's change that!

Sometimes achieving this shift in attitude takes some serious soul-searching. Something's got to give. But nowadays you can't pick up a *Good Housekeeping* magazine or watch Martha Stewart without feeling like you're just not doing enough: "Home-Cooked Meals in Under Ten Minutes!" "Quickie Organizing: Energize Your Home!" or "How to Raise Your

KATRIN'S CHRISTMAS LETTER FROM HELL

Here's a confession: I *like* getting those long-winded Christmas letters once a year. And because I have a lot of family and friends abroad, I've sent out holiday cards every year since before I even graduated from college. I never missed one—not even the year when I was stuck in a dirt hole in Africa for a month over Christmas.

Once I started having kids, I included an annual letter. Writing it was really fun: I grew up in England, where irony is an art form, but I still managed to pat myself on the back (subtly, of course) and make sure to relay the various exciting things that were happening to me and my ever-growing family.

Eventually we stopped moving so much, and there was a lot less thrilling stuff to write about. Some friends of my husband, Kevin, from business school had already started retiring, and my life didn't seem even vaguely glamorous anymore. Oh, and of course I couldn't claim a piano prodigy or an Olympic skater among my brood; mine were just, well, *ordinary* kids.

So what was I going to share with all these friends about our life? I'm a compulsively honest person, and my instinct was to send out a big wail to the universe: Help! Life isn't the way I thought it would be!

I thought long and hard about that letter. Finally, I opened it by declaring the most important lesson I'd learned that year: You do the best you can. The next year rolled around. Life was insane: a big move from the west to the east coast, a premature birth, and a slump in my creative life. So I gave myself permission to skip my annual letter.

Next year? Hmmm. I could skip that one too, couldn't I? After all, the world hadn't stopped turning the year before.

I can't tell you what a huge relief it was for me to decide that I didn't need to send those letters every single year any-more. If I don't have time, don't feel like it, don't have anything great to share, then to hell with it! What a glorious liberation from the tyranny of passing inspection each and every year.

Child's I.Q." When everyone's telling us to try harder, do more, improve, build, and grow, it's hard to shrug it off.

We have yet to meet a mother who doesn't strive to be a better parent. Every woman we interviewed felt she could still find ways to improve her parenting skills. But there are some major differences between *perfectionism*, which is clearly destructive, and *striving*, which is normal and constructive. Healthy striving is when:

> ► We set goals based on our own standards, shaking off the yoke of others' expectations.

▶ We set goals that are one step beyond what we've already achieved—they're worth reaching for, but they're also achievable.

▶ We derive pleasure from the *process* of running our lives, and we understand that it's not all about the end result.

▶ When there is failure or a setback, criticism by others or imposed on ourselves does not diminish our feelings of self-worth.

Success is the ability to go from one failure to another with no loss of enthusiasm.
—Sir Winston Churchill, former British prime minister

FROM PROBLEM TO SOLUTION

Nicole, Mother of Three from California

Nicole has never worked outside the home and loves focusing her energies on her family. In her neighborhood, many women once had careers but now work part-time or stay at home. They fill their every spare minute with activities, while Nicole prefers to keep it simple. "I was constantly looking around at other moms, worrying I was missing something," she said. Then she started observing something important: as her kids grew up, they were becoming remarkably independent and self-motivated. "That's when I realized I could only be myself, and that was just fine."

ANNE'S QUIRKY GARDEN

My next-door neighbor has beautiful gardens that I've always admired. For years I've watched a small embankment by my driveway grow more and more out of control. I always had the best intentions, but it just seemed too daunting to launch in. Also, I had the rest of the yard to worry about, and believe me, that's not a thing of beauty!

One Saturday in early spring I got my courage up and started to dig. I decided that anything would be better than a sea of weeds. Before I knew it, the kids joined in. I declared to my husband, Bruce, that he was in charge of the rest of the yard, but this was *my* baby.

With the kids involved here and there throughout the day, we mixed in bags and bags of new soil, and planted annuals and perennials. It was physically exhausting, but so satisfying. By the end of the weekend, the spot looked clean and neat with a few flowers dotted around. In the spare moments throughout the rest of the week, we planted a little more. There it was: our first garden!

Slowly, life took over, and I started to notice that some of my "babies" weren't doing so well. I tried desperately to bring them back to life, but to no avail. By the end of the summer, the garden looked pretty sad, but the kids saw only beauty. They would constantly comment on how big the flowers had become and how much they liked the pink one or the blue one. "Look at our garden, Mom!" my daughter would say as we pulled in the driveway. Our quirky garden was the best we could do, and we really loved it. It was through this process that I realized that I didn't need the perfect garden; I just needed to enjoy getting my hands dirty and bonding with my kids.

Throughout the year, I've tried to translate this experience to other areas of our life—it's not always going to be what the neighbor next door is doing, but it works for us.

The Attitude Shift

If trying to be the perfect mother is self-defeating, then how do we avoid it? It's all about our outlook. Changing ingrained mental habits takes true courage. It's uncomfortable to feel that your standards may be lower than others. It'll probably make you uneasy to admit to yourself that you're consciously looking for ways to cut corners. Most likely, you'll hear that old enemy, guilt, knocking at your door when you go lie on the couch instead of clearing the dinner dishes.

The value of *intention* is often given short shrift in our modern, do-it-all culture. Just because you don't achieve perfect results, or even moderate success, doesn't automatically mean the effort was wasted. You try and try, and maybe you succeed, maybe not. That's what real life is really like.

We can tone down the self-imposed pressure by learning to let go, but we can also work on *enjoying* the mess and unpredictability of real life. Sounds impossible, and for some of us it is. But of all the women we've talked with, the ones who seemed most content with their lives are the ones who found real joy in the midst of the chaos.

> Whatever is flexible and loving will tend to grow; whatever is rigid and blocked will wither and die.
> —Lao-tzu, Chinese philosopher

Mothers say it's important to:

▶ **Accept imperfection, perhaps even revel in it.** Joelle, mother of one from New York, loves going to her messy friend's house. It reminds her that not everyone has to live with the same standards.

▶ **Share responsibility, and let go of the need to always be in control.** When your nine-year-old folds laundry, tell her you appreciate how hard he or she tried.

▶ **Open your mind to alternative ways of running things.** Elizabeth, raised in Germany and now living with her family of five in France, noticed how differently even those two neighboring cultures can be when it comes to mothers' standards. "There's no one way to do it correctly," she said. "It really helps me to know that."

As a kid, you probably loved getting drenched in the rain or having your hands covered in paint. Maybe you lay on your bed giggling with a friend, having the time of your life, oblivious to whether your room was a mess or not. As long as you felt loved and had curiosity about the world, you were content. If you can find this joy as an adult, regardless of the outer trappings of life, you'll be golden.

> *Perfectionism is self-abuse of the highest order.*
> —Anne Wilson Schaef, writer

TIPS FROM THE TRENCHES

▶ **Observe yourself closely.** Each morning for one week, write a list of your expectations for the day in your *Woman's Workbook*. At the end of the day, sit down for a few minutes with your list. Did you achieve what you set out to achieve? If not, why not? Was your goal impossible? Was the outcome out of your control? Is it possible that had you worded that goal differently, you wouldn't see your efforts as a failure? Make a list of everything you *did* do. It's probably a lot more than you give yourself credit for.

▶ **Cut to the chase.** Think of some things that make you feel great—activities, images, words, or memories. Find old photos, and write things down. How many of those things are dependent on being perfect? We'll bet many of your favorite moments are snapshots of an ordinary life where things don't always go according to plan.

▶ **Experiment with loosening the reins.** If you can't leave the house without making the beds, experiment for one week with not doing them. If this makes you too anxious, try eliminating another optional task from your list. Do the kids always have to wear clean clothes *every day*? Try letting them wear the same pants, but changing their underwear and shirt. Do you feel bad if they don't get a bath or shower each night? Adopt a three-or-four-times-a-week rule. This will help you learn to let go a bit.

▶ **Pay attention to your self-talk.** When your mind starts telling you things like: "Oh-oh, that was bad. How could I mess that up?" or "Why am I the only mom who can't seem to get the laundry done *and* her kids to bed?" say out loud, "Enough already! I *deserve* a time-out from self-criticism!" Change this "self-talk" from negative to positive.

▶ **Play the "What if . . . ?" game.** Find a few friends you trust in your community or at work. Perhaps you're part of a book group and can bring along this book. Maybe you have a church group open to discussing personal issues. Take turns thinking about the things that you insist on doing, and doing *just so*; then play the "What if . . . ?" game. What would happen if I stopped checking my daughter's homework? What if I didn't lose ten pounds by Christmas (or summer)? What if I skipped the meeting about my son's music performance?

▶ **Find new priorities.** There are things that we must do, things we want to do, and things we think we have to do. Learning to distinguish between these will free you up. Get a big piece of paper. Decide if you want to tackle one week at a time or one month. Make three headings: "Must Do," "Want to Do," "Should Do." Split your goals into those three columns. At the end of the week or month, determine whether you've been content or frazzled. Did you put something in the wrong column? Did you give too much attention to the "should dos"? Take a big black pen, and *cross something off the list.*

▶ **Delegate and appreciate.** Household chores have to get done. If you're doing a lot of the work yourself, ask why. Could it be that you think you do it better, quicker, more to your specifications than anyone else? Learn to let go. When your kids unload the dishwasher or fold laundry, it's OK for the job to be done their way. If your husband makes dinner, let him be the boss. And remember to notice and appreciate the help you do get.

▶ **Say no more often.** It is so hard for some of us to say no. We don't like to say no to our kids, our friends, our bosses. The only person we feel comfortable saying no to is ourselves. The next time your gut tells you that you don't want to do something—sign up for a task, put your kid on a new team, host a dinner, whatever—just say no! Practice an excuse, if it makes you feel more comfortable, or even better, just say, "Sorry, I can't this time," or "Let me sleep on it." But be firm.

▶ **Take one step at a time.** Maybe you have certain standards that can't be lowered—for example, family dinners really matter to you. But you find it's not enough to have everyone gathered at least three times a week, the table looking great, and the meals home cooked. Maybe you find yourself getting tense while preparing dinner, and you sit through it feeling irritated that no one's appreciating the moment. Try toning your one important priority down a notch. Sit together over a take-out meal once in a while—using nice plates and napkins.

▶ **Analyze your past.** Think back to your most wonderful childhood memory. Is it when you got a star on that science paper (which your parents helped you rewrite)? Probably not. Is it that you lived in a tidy, impeccably decorated house? Most likely, the things you remember most dearly about being a kid have nothing to do with how much effort your mother put into the job of mothering. We'll bet that your very best images are simple: sitting curled up with your mom reading, playing for hours on end with cardboard boxes, watching your parents laugh. Just thinking about those images will make you smile.

I TRIED THE TIPS! SALLY, MOTHER OF FOUR FROM MASSACHUSETTS

"You know, I'm always behind the eight ball, so I tried the new priorities suggestion—the columns and all. Right away, I found that there were things on my list that were just not realistic, such as the birthday present I missed buying a year ago, so I crossed them off forever. Also, I plugged some of my top priorities into my calendar, like renewing my license and getting new windshield wipers. The best thing of all is that I could transfer some of my to-dos onto other people in my family. So I'm also learning to let go!"

THE POWER OF SELF-AWARENESS

From Losing Yourself in Motherhood to Understanding Who You Are Today

We were sitting in a big circle on the floor during one of our early focus groups. A dozen mothers—some of whom knew each other, but many who didn't—were sharing stories. Our topic was big. It was huge. It was all-encompassing. It was "Losing Yourself in Motherhood."

The evening came to an end, but the women continued talking.

It got later and later.

They just kept going.

*Happiness is when what you think, what you say,
and what you do are in harmony.*
—Mahatma Gandhi, former leader of India

One story after another, each one revealing greater, harder truths. There was no holding back. These women had so much to say and so many questions to ask each other, it was as if a dam had burst.

The water roared around us, and we settled in for the ride, all the while scribbling furiously. In talking about self-awareness—in a comfortable environment, among other women right in the motherhood trenches—we would touch on every theme in the book.

The Invisible Woman

Have you ever:

- ▶ Rushed to get your children out of the house in the mornings, only to discover upon arriving at work that you put your underpants on backward?
- ▶ Returned home after food shopping to find you bought hot dogs and frozen pizza and snack packs, but no food for yourself?
- ▶ Headed off on a vacation laden with gadgets, books, and CDs for your kids, but no novel for you to enjoy because—what's the point, anyway?
- ▶ Been at a loss for words at a dinner party, when you can't think of a single engaging thing to talk about with your fascinating, well-traveled, child-free neighbor?
- ▶ Listened to "friends" in the carpool line or at the bus stop talking about their genius children and worried silently about how you let the ball drop?

▶ Found yourself agreeing to something you totally disagree with, because you're too tired or overwhelmed to stand up for yourself even though *you're* the adult and *they're* the kids?

For it is surely a lifetime work, this learning to be a woman.
—May Sarton, poet

When you first became a mother, you probably thought—just as we did—that you could have and do it all, only to discover that you lost sight of yourself somewhere along the way. Maybe now that both you and your kids are older, you're wondering what happened to your energy, your optimism, and your sense of control. Almost every mother in that early focus group and in later discussions admitted how surprised she was to find herself so stressed and overwhelmed long after her children were out of diapers. These women thought or hoped that the feeling that they'd put their own lives on hold would just go away. But it didn't.

We've signed up for this job for life! So our feeling is, let's make sure we not only do it well, but enjoy it too.

To keep a lamp burning we have to keep putting oil in it.
—Mother Teresa, missionary

In their heart of hearts, mothers know their needs matter; they're just so conditioned to be caretakers that they forget to treat *themselves* with compassion and respect. Psychologist Dr. Helene G. Brenner, author of *I Know I'm in There Somewhere*, says, "Almost all women live their lives standing outside themselves, always ready to judge their bodies, their feelings, and their thoughts from an external standard and find themselves wanting." By accepting that your thoughts and needs are as valid as the thoughts and needs of the people you love, and by giving yourself permission to take time-outs, you'll be on the road to rediscovering your sense of self.

You're in the Driver's Seat

Without exception, every mother we talked with spoke about her life in terms of work *before* kids and work *after* kids. Mothers defined themselves more by the paid work they did or still do than by what interests they pursue, what moves them, and what they want to talk about every moment they get a chance. Why is this, we wondered?

> *In the middle of difficulty lies opportunity.*
> —Albert Einstein, scientist

We think it goes back to how modern women measure themselves and how they determine their values. As we all know too well, success at motherhood is basically impossible to define or achieve, and so we search for other ways to feel validated. As a consequence, many moms make themselves even busier with work or chores, trying to get on top of things, all the while los-

FROM PROBLEM TO SOLUTION

Trisha, Mother of Three from Connecticut

When we met Trisha, she was feeling pretty good. But it hadn't always been that way. Four years earlier, when she quit her job to focus on her kids, the transition was much harder than she'd ever imagined. "I was so bored," she said, "and I felt guilty all the time. But raising your kids, you don't get a do-over!" Eventually her husband couldn't stand her sad face any longer; he encouraged her to take classes or go to a therapist to figure out why she was so miserable. As an experiment, Trisha started working part-time at the community theater in town and found she had a passion for movies. "I've rediscovered my zest for life," she said. "I don't know where it's going to take me, but I've never felt better!"

ing touch with the sense of purpose they felt when they pursued activities they cared deeply about.

Truth be told, we're the only ones responsible for our own happiness. Think about how you spend your time compared to how you would *like* to spend your time. Work, kids, teachers, home, groceries, laundry, family, friends, commutes, doctors—you name the activity and you're probably doing it. Can you identify what's holding you back from fitting into your life those moments that actually fill you up? We'll bet that you've determined there just aren't enough hours in the day.

> *Take your life in your own hands and what happens?*
> *A terrible thing: no one to blame.*
> —Erica Jong, writer

You'd be surprised by how often it's simply the *perception* that change is impossible that holds mothers back. Lily from Virginia, mother of three, explained it this way: "I stubbornly hold to the idea that I don't have time for anything but work and family. I'm always taking things away, not adding!" But we've learned that most of the time all it takes is a small shift to start getting back to what you love. Lily loved yoga but just couldn't fit it in anymore. She missed it so much, she started doing a single headstand in the mornings, eventually carving out fifteen minutes every day to do some asanas.

The first step is identifying what makes you feel connected, and the second is carving out little pockets of time to help that feeling grow. Take it one headstand at a time.

> *Self-knowledge is the great power by which*
> *we comprehend and control our lives.*
> —Vernon Howard, philosopher

But what if you have no idea what turns you on? Caitlin from Massachusetts, mother of two, said, "I'm a giver—always thinking of others before myself. My husband will say, 'Do what you want,' and I just don't know. I'm still trying to sort out what makes me feel good, but I'm happy to be working on it."

FROM PROBLEM TO SOLUTION

Channing, Mother of One from Vermont

Channing always loved photography. Her son Jake is autistic, and her husband's salary is dependent on bonuses, so Channing works a demanding job and has little time for herself. She had long ago given up the pipe dream of becoming a professional photographer. But the urge to be creative just kept tugging at her. "I started snapping pictures everywhere I went, even though I didn't have any particular plan or strategy," she explained. "But that was enough to make me feel like me again." Now she occasionally takes pictures for her local paper and at least gets to pretend she's a semipro.

Peeling Back the Layers to Uncover the Real You

Just as the word *selfish* turns most mothers off, so do notions like "finding your inner voice" or "staying centered." Karen, a mother of four from Texas, told us that whenever she hears expressions like that, she tunes out. "Do I have time to be all yogalike? I'm juggling a job and teenagers; it bothers me to be preached at." You don't have to buy into these abstract notions wholesale, but there's just no way around it: without understanding what makes you tick, you just won't have any energy or goodwill left to give to those you love.

ANNE LISTENS TO HER GUT

For as long as I can remember, I've worked. From babysitting, to hostessing at a local restaurant, to being a lifeguard—I was just one of those kids who always had a job. I loved the camaraderie, the way work set the rhythm of my week, and exposing myself to different experiences. Not to mention that earning money didn't hurt.

When I first became a mom, life was no different. After my maternity leave, I headed into town to a part-time job in human resources. I remember telling a colleague, "I can't believe they *pay* me for this; I feel like I'm on vacation!" I swear you could have seen skid marks as I'd peel out of the driveway on Monday mornings. On the flip side, as I was coming home, I'd be racing down the highway to see my twin girls Carly and Meg again after being away for so many hours.

I kept working until my third child, Jay, was a year old. Then the company I worked for was sold, my position was eliminated, and I was home full-time. I was pretty excited: I'd have more time to let the days unfold with my kids! I could do things for myself!

But with the demands of parenting twenty-four hours a day, seven days a week, I quickly realized that I desperately needed to get out of my own four walls and to find something just for me.

First, I took up running. Three mornings a week I'd meet my running partners and off we'd go. Soon one mile led to another, and the next thing we knew we were running marathons. But still I needed more. I tried tennis, yoga, and golf, and I filled my days with volunteer activities. This was all exciting at first, but I soon realized it wasn't really the way I wanted to spend my time. One time I stood on a tennis court, in the middle of play, and thought to myself, "What on God's green earth am I doing here?"

Then one day I commented enviously to a mom passing by, dressed for work, "You're so lucky." She did a double take and said, "We should talk!"

Shortly thereafter, I was back at work. On one of my first days in the office, the feeling that I was in the right place overtook me. It was in that moment that I knew at my very core that working in the city, and all that it brings to my life, was the very thing that I'd been missing all along. I must admit, there are days when I catch myself daydreaming about the life of the stay-at-home mom, but listening to my gut leads me back to the office week after week.

We asked some mothers to write down for us their definition of self-awareness, right off the top of their heads. Here are a few they came up with:

► It's the ability to reflect and adapt.

► It's knowing what really makes you tick.

► It's when you understand your motives.

► It's when you're paying attention and are *not* in reaction mode.

► It's about understanding what you need and being able to articulate that to others.

> People often say that this or that person has not yet found himself. But the self is not something one finds, it is something one creates.
> —Thomas S. Szasz, psychiatrist

Life coach Betsy Cole, who works with individuals and corporations to help them better define themselves and their needs, sees self-awareness as "the personal understanding of the very core of one's identity." It's about being both mentally and physically present, and understanding the deep connection between your physical state and your emotional state of being. So for instance, if you have stomach cramps or a painful jaw, you connect the dots by examining what emotional circumstances in your life might be causing stress.

So in a way, self-awareness is the very opposite of being on autopilot. It's the state we achieve when we've examined our motivation and have decided to act upon our needs. Greater awareness brings recognition of choice, which in turn enables change and leads to greater freedom.

FROM PROBLEM TO SOLUTION

Maya, Mother of Two from Australia

One of Maya's girls recently joined a swimming class that takes place in the early evening, right when Maya's usually making dinner for the family. After a month or two of this new routine, Maya started feeling disgruntled and at first couldn't figure out why. So she tried to pay attention to exactly what she was feeling and when she felt it. "I realized how much I *love* cooking; how much that special quiet time in the kitchen and then the togetherness in the evening means to me," she said. Now she knows that as the girls get older she has to either schedule their activities earlier in the day so she can do her thing, or she has to find something else that fills her up in the same way.

The very first step in becoming more self-aware is remarkably simple: *pause.* Just stop for a moment. Take a time-out! Observe what's going on inside yourself, and then ask why it's happening. Janet, mother of two from California, said if she starts grinding her teeth, she knows she's about to be sarcastic and mean with her kids. "I know how it escalates; I really know my triggers," she said, "and I just don't want to go there. So I stop!"

Mothers have many different ways of achieving greater insight—the three of us are certainly a testament to that. If you think you might like experimenting with writing down your thoughts, grab your *Woman's Workbook* and start scribbling like Susan does. Sally, entrepreneur from Texas and mother of one, told us she started by writing down just a single word for each day. Although she was always pressed for time, the process of picking that one word to represent her day encouraged her to take a moment to reflect on her life.

> *Success means having the courage, the determination and the will to become the person you believe you were meant to be.*
> —George Sheehan, philosopher

Anne runs outdoors, trying to feel the connection between her feet and the earth beneath them. This approach to introspection through physical activity and observing nature was a favorite of many mothers. All expressed that breathing in the fresh air, doing something repetitive and calming, while working their bodies helped them get in touch with themselves. Even when physical activity outdoors isn't possible, being still and observing nature can lead to the serenity that encourages self-examination. Marta, mother of two from Italy, lives in a city apartment, but often goes to the river when she needs peace. "I can stare at the water, the movement," she says, "and find the space to think."

As a way to tune out the noises of everyday life, visual thinkers like Katrin often focus on pictures and objects, or engage in a creative activity. Some write affirmations, placing them in a highly visible spot, such as above the bathroom mirror, in the car, or near the computer. Many artistically inclined moms make pottery, paint, sculpt, sew, or draw. They find that the process of creating something with their hands allows them to clear their minds and live in the moment with greater awareness.

> *Writing crystallizes thought and produces action.*
> —Paul J. Meyer, writer

This kind of peaceful introspection is so beneficial to the hurried woman. It can:

- ► Build self-knowledge, and therefore also self-confidence
- ► Help you identify your values by clarifying thought processes and stripping away learned behavior
- ► Put you back in touch with your instincts, which will also make decisions come more easily
- ► Push you, gently, from intention to action
- ► Release pent-up emotions or fears that might otherwise crowd your days with negative energy

Everyone's different, and so each journey will take different routes. But here are some tips we gathered over the years that are applicable to every woman hoping to get in better touch with her needs:

▶ **Be patient.** Answers to the elusive question *why* you feel a certain way may take a while in coming: if you find yourself becoming frustrated quickly, just give it time.

▶ **Be compassionate.** Instead of always trying to change yourself, try being more accepting. For instance, if you're always late, instead of beating yourself up about it, tell people with a smile, "Sorry, I'm often running five minutes behind schedule, but you can count on me to always turn up!"

▶ **Take responsibility.** Avoid blaming others or circumstances for what's holding you back. It's *not* too late, you're *not* too old, and money's *not* the answer to every problem. Recognize that you have the power to make choices, one by one, that can lead you toward greater happiness.

▶ **Listen to your instincts.** Trust what your gut is telling you, and tune out the distracting noises—the expectations of others—that swirl around you.

> *Be patient toward all that is unsolved in your heart*
> *and try to love the questions themselves.*
> —Rainer Maria Rilke, poet

Feeling Connected

In the process of examining yourself and the way you run your life (i.e., as you become more self-aware), you'll uncover your passions, your deepest fears, and your greatest needs. You'll become aware of some of the habits you've fallen into that are

FROM PROBLEM TO SOLUTION

Anna, Mother of Two from Rhode Island

Anna loved knitting when she was a teenager. When she got married and became a mother, she stayed at home for some years and enjoyed the flexibility of being there for her family. But she *hated* the financial dependence. "I realized that I really needed to make some money, and I tapped into my old passion—knitting!" she explained. She started making knit handbags and now runs a thriving small business. "It makes all the difference to me to participate financially, and I can't believe I also get to do what I love."

counterproductive. But most wonderful of all, you'll start to live a more authentic and connected life, according to your own convictions. In the novel *The Hitchhiker's Guide to the Galaxy* by Douglas Adams, a character says, "He felt that his whole life was some kind of dream and he sometimes wondered whose it was and whether they were enjoying it."

Haven't we all felt that way from time to time? As though we aren't really masters of our own destiny? As though we have lost our connection with the people and the world we love? Well, once you pay more attention to what your soul craves— by being a little *more* self-centered—you can start reclaiming ownership of your life.

SUSAN AND HER SOLITARY SEARCH

One night soon after my third child, Hugh, was born, I had just settled him into his bassinet and the house was perfectly still. As I often did during nights like those, I pondered my choices in life, such as the one I'd just made to leave my full-time job. I'd thought the decision through, but I was feeling very unsure of where I would find the challenges I needed to keep me happy. Maybe I'd start hiking, I thought, or bike in a race. Or what if I went on Outward Bound—a trip I'd wanted to do my whole life?

The following year, I decided to go on an eight-day kayaking trip in the Ten Thousand Islands in Florida. I trained so hard that I was sore all over, but psyched. We kayaked vigorously, and we talked and listened. We learned how to do a 360 in the boats, and we read poetry and shared stories. My daily journal entries started shifting toward lofty questions like, "Who am I?" "Why do I want to challenge myself?" "What is my purpose?" and "What makes me happy?"

I didn't have any answers yet.

Then my solo trip came along. The team dropped me off on one of the islands, alone. I had a spit of a beach, all one hundred yards of it to myself. The mosquitoes were swarming, so I started walking back and forth, back and forth, for three hours. Then I sat with my journal for four more hours. As each hour passed, I was more and more at peace. Those journal entries would be a testament to one of the most pivotal moments in my life.

I started to realize how deeply I enjoyed being a mom and how much I did not miss having demanding clients. The diverse set of people I met on that trip had catapulted me into a new way of seeing myself. For the first time I could truly be myself: the listener, the mother, the caregiver, the sensitive one, the dreamer, the optimist, the controller, and the helper. In letting me be me, I found comfort in my strengths and I accepted my weaknesses. That night crystallized what was important to me: family, learning, having an outside passion, and living with gratitude.

At this point, we can guess what you're thinking: so what exactly distinguishes destructive self-indulgence from constructive selfishness?

Passion!

Think back to when you were younger, how much passion you felt for—pick your thing—art, hiking, writing, movies, music, sports, plays, charitable causes, work, travel, friends, animals, or children. Passion, which is the energy and dedication that comes from really caring about an activity, was a part of our lives that most of us took for granted. But it's what made us feel a deep sense of connection between ourselves and the life we were living.

"But I was just a baby then!" you skeptically say to yourself. "What did I know about endless routines, unacknowledged sacrifices, relentless responsibilities, or unpredictable outcomes? Things are different now. For starters, I don't have time for passion!"

> *The essentials to happiness are something to love,*
> *something to do, and something to hope for.*
> —William Blake, poet

Life without a sense of drive and meaning can get monotonous pretty quickly. All human beings need motivation, affirmation, and a feeling of pride and success. Solana, mother of three from Massachusetts, explained that after staying at home for a while with her babies, she realized she needed to "do something with my brain because when I did, and when I was together with my kids, I could be nice to them again!" She sets herself a goal of reading one book every month.

A 2005 Harris Interactive Poll showed that only 20 percent of Americans feel passionate about what they do—and this state of affairs is even worse for mothers, whether they work outside the home or not. The Cincinnati Children's Hospital Medical Center conducted a study in 2003 of mothers who brought their kids into the emergency room for nonthreatening problems. Thirty percent of those moms screened positive for depression, anxiety, panic attacks, or physical problems related to stress!

> *We are all so very unique. What a precious gift the world loses if we don't find out who we are and then share our individuality.*
>
> **—Joan Anderson, writer**

Once you've paused to hear that quiet inner voice whispering what it needs, you can begin making the choices necessary to turn those wishes into reality. Ask yourself these questions, and write down your answers in your *Woman's Workbook*, remembering that you may not have all the answers right away:

- ▶ What gives you goosebumps?
- ▶ What could you chatter about incessantly?
- ▶ What do you want to learn more about?
- ▶ What or who do you want to feel more connected to?
- ▶ What do you do that simply feels right?

The Power of Positive Thinking

If you believe you can do something, you probably can; if you're filled with self-doubt, you probably can't. In her book, *Let Your Goddess Grow*, Dr. Charlene Proctor says that the way you *think* about the world and your role in it is what creates your own reality. That may sound a little nutty, but in doing all our research we came to believe that positive thinking can actually be the key to unlocking a person's full potential. "It doesn't take any technical expertise. We must simply be strong enough to choose what we want to experience," Proctor writes. "All of a sudden we notice we have created a fabulous reality based upon our intentions."

Here are some techniques that helped the mothers who shared them with us focus on the positive:

- ► Rephrase negative thoughts. Instead of thinking, "I'm never going to get through this," think, "I'll certainly feel great when I get through this!"
- ► Try not to personalize criticism: rather than interpreting a comment as related to your failings, take them at face value. "The pasta is cold," is not the same as "You're a bad cook."
- ► Be active so you can shake yourself out of a negative mode. Or do the exact opposite and be completely still. Expel those bad vibes.
- ► Practice meditation or pray.
- ► Break challenges into small, manageable chunks.
- ► Accept that practice makes perfect, and mastery takes time. Every failure is actually an opportunity to learn.
- ► Try not to project today's setbacks into future disappointments. Unfortunately, pessimism tends to be self-fulfilling.

FROM PROBLEM TO SOLUTION

Elaine, Mother of Three from California

As a freelance writer, Elaine was always suffering rejections. She'd pitch a story and invariably get just as many nos as yeses from editors. "It was really hard on my psyche," she said, "because I started feeling like I just wasn't good enough." So instead of focusing on her nonfiction work all the time, she started working on a novel late at night after everyone was asleep. "It's crazy, but as soon as I opened myself up to possibilities, it seemed like good things started to happen." The newfound energy for her writing translated into fun human-interest stories that she started selling.

> *The worst loneliness is not to be comfortable with yourself.*
> —Mark Twain, writer

What if you're facing more than just doubts or negative self-talk? Many women are confronted with major challenges in their lives, not just small bumps in the road. We've talked to moms who have seriously disabled children, who've lost their husbands, who live with debilitating illnesses, or who have had the rug pulled out from under them financially. Dr. Jon Kabat-Zinn of the University of Massachusetts Medical School explains in the book *The Mindful Way Through Depression* that a "shift in per-

KATRIN MINES THE DEPTHS

A few years ago, I took my son Peter to the Museum of
Fine Arts on Saturdays for art class. I loved those hours
wandering in solitude among the paintings; with Svenja just
a newborn and Greta a super-cranky toddler, it was the
only peace I could find in the middle of my hectic days. I
was really missing Europe and city life. I'd given up a job
producing for radio and was trying to finish my first novel.
I often spent this museum time scribbling in my writer's
notebook. This is an entry I made that led me to start
reevaluating the choices I was making about how I spent
my time:

    *I remember going to the Jeu de Paume gallery when I
was a teenager. The art spoke to me so clearly, it contained
so much of the mystery of the world—history, people,
relationships, and the mind's ability to concentrate, work,
and put together something beautiful. Now I'm all grown
up, and I wonder how I can be in charge of so many
people and their happiness when I myself am so empty.*

    *What will it take to make me feel more real? Why can't
I be content with what I have? What do I really want? I feel
as though everyone and everything feeds off me.*

    That day I went home and cried bitterly. I admitted
how I was feeling to my husband, Kevin, even though I
couldn't pinpoint *why* I felt that way. Then I decided to take

action. I wrote three lists and filled them in. The lists had the following titles:

1. I Don't Want
2. I Need
3. To Do as Soon as Possible!

I understood that I couldn't expect my life to be handed to me on a silver platter—I had to *make* it happen. I realized that I really missed people and that I had to find a way to interact more with others. I started going to book readings and signed up for some evening classes. Then I took it even farther: I launched private writing workshops, and soon I had a small freelance editing business. By making small changes, one by one, I eventually wrestled back a sense of self-control.

spective toward our thoughts and feelings, as well as how they express themselves in our bodies and our lives, allows us to face life's challenges with far greater resilience."

Mothers agreed: when you suffer major setbacks, it's important to acknowledge the pain and frustration and then work toward moving on. Irene is a mother of two from Delaware who lost both her parents in one year. "I pushed aside my anger, thinking I needed to move ahead," she said. "Then I realized I was on a razor's edge—kind of losing it."

"Healing yourself comes in two stages," explains Deepak Chopra in his book *The Deeper Wound*, "first releasing the energy of suffering, then replacing it with the soul's energy." Positive energy comes from surrounding yourself with thoughts that *support* your belief in yourself and in the goodness of the world.

> You gain strength, courage, and confidence by every experience in which you really stop to look fear in the face.
> —Eleanor Roosevelt, former First Lady

So if positive statements result in positive feelings, which then enable progress, try completing the following three statements, including as many optimistic and accurate descriptors as possible:

- ▶ I am . . .
- ▶ I can . . .
- ▶ I will . . .

This will help you visualize the possibilities that are already inherent in your life. "Each limit exceeded, each boundary crossed, verifies that most limits are self-imposed, that your potential and possibilities are far greater than you have imagined, and that you are capable of far more than you thought," says Robert Kriegel, former Olympic coach in his book *Sacred*

Cows Make the Best Burgers. Instead of focusing on the hurdles, picture the meandering track ahead and put on your running shoes. Rid yourself of heavy emotional baggage, and give yourself the permission to grow and change as much or as little as you need to.

> *The only way to make sense out of change is to plunge with it, move with it, and join the dance.*
> —Alan Watts, comparative religion expert

The Journey Has Begun

Parents have a big job, there's no doubt about it. No one wants to fail at this massive undertaking, when it's clearly the most important thing any of us could ever do. Ask yourself this: If your life as a woman feels balanced and calm, won't your life as a mother be all that much better? And won't your children and your spouse feel the love?

As you continue to think about how to bring greater self-awareness into your life, ask yourself these basic questions every now and then:

- ► Are you able to identify what makes you tick? Are you willing to try?
- ► Do you have things in your life that you find beautiful?
- ► Does your imagination have an outlet?
- ► Are you learning something new everyday?

- Do you follow your instinct and allow yourself to be spontaneous?
- Are you kind, forgiving, and patient with yourself?
- Do you believe that you have choices?

By continuing to take these steps toward a more authentic life—acknowledging that a little selfishness goes a long way—you've launched yourself on the journey toward a happier life.

> The purpose of life is to live it, to taste experience to the utmost, to reach out eagerly and without fear for newer and richer experience.
> —Eleanor Roosevelt, former First Lady

TIPS FROM THE TRENCHES

- **Make a declaration.** Sometimes what we need is some firmness and determination. Once you've figured out some things you'd like to change about your life, some traits in yourself you'd like to downplay or to focus on, make a serious declaration of your intent. You may say: "I am going to spend one evening each week painting; I will change my habit of waking up tired and grumpy; I will not react so quickly to my children."
- **Step outside yourself.** Try having an out-of-body experience so you can see your patterns of behavior, reactions,

and thought processes more objectively. Life coaches say you should imagine you're standing behind your real self, looking over your shoulder. It's as though you're a scientist collecting data for future use. Observe when you're uncomfortable, when you're having difficult conversations, and when you're happy. You'll free yourself from limiting habits by discovering some of your triggers.

▶ **Write daily pages.** Many creativity coaches and therapists encourage writing as a way of tapping into your subconscious. We love Julia Cameron's idea of writing what she calls "Morning Pages" each and every day. This is when you wake up and before doing anything else, you write down everything you can think of until you've filled three pages. Even when you have nothing to write about, you'll be amazed at what will pop up into your consciousness.

▶ **Reposition your priorities.** Get seven index cards, and write one of the following words on each card: Mind, Body, Spirit, Family, Friends, Work, Relationship. Lay them out on the floor in front of you. Place them in the order of how much time and energy you dedicate to each one. Does the order reflect the way you want to be spending your time? On the right-hand side of the card, write down what you currently enjoy about each of these parts of your life, and on the left-hand side, write what you need to nourish more.

▶ **Be daring.** Think big. Instead of hoping to have a poem published, plan on getting your novel out there. Rather than dreaming of a night away from your family, work toward taking a sabbatical from work, finding a new class to take, or starting your own business on the side. These kinds of big ideas may seem intimidating at first, but you can train yourself to believe in their potential.

▶ **Use your body as a sensor.** When your heart is pounding or your mouth is dry, when you're exhausted or your hands are shaking, there's often an external event that is affecting your emotions and expressing itself through your physical discomfort. Doctors say you should take note of how your body reacts to certain situations, so you can begin to identify those that make you feel bad, and then change or avoid them.

▶ **Find a blast from the past.** We all have memories of being a child and having a moment of intense happiness; and usually the catalyst was something small, such as an incredible sunset, a dog's lick, an ice cream cone from a quiet uncle, or the frigid water of a lake. Write down ten things that made you happy as a child. Can you do any of those ten things again as an adult? In the coming month, or week, or day?

▶ **Identify symbols of happiness.** Flowers make some women really happy. Others love thick bath towels. One woman with three kids, Savanna, loves the smell of sharpened pencils. What are the everyday things that bring a smile to your face? Make sure to have those things in your home. When you're feeling down or confused, take yourself away from where you are and go touch that object. Spend a good few minutes observing it, and then move on.

▶ **Vent in an unsent letter.** Let's just purge those feelings of anger or jealousy we lug around with us like a ball and chain. Sit down and write a letter to someone you're really angry at: maybe it's your seventh-grade teacher who made you feel stupid, or your father who didn't allow you to become a vet; it could be your child who never listens, or your boss who treats you like a servant. Get it all out on paper in no uncertain terms. Then burn it—and never look back.

▶ **Recognize what's in front of you.** Instead of simply gliding through your day operating in your comfort zone, according to your habitual assumptions about people or events, try opening yourself up to possibilities that present themselves to you without you even noticing. When you get an invitation from left field that you would usually turn down without a second thought, try embracing it instead. Maybe going to the art show with your old roommate or on the nature hike with your second grader will offer up a moment of beauty that is all the more satisfying because it's entirely unexpected.

▶ **Clarify your goals.** Sometimes the biggest challenge is discovering what your own personal goals actually are. A great way to start this process is to carve out some alone time with your *Woman's Workbook* and start making some lists, such as "What do I want?" "What do I *not* want?" "What do I like about my life right now?" "What don't I like about my life so much?" Realizing that you have choices to make and being honest with yourself will help you believe you really can make your goals a reality.

I TRIED THE TIPS! JEN, MOTHER OF TWO FROM GEORGIA

"I never thought of myself as a writer, but when I'm tense I like to doodle, so I thought I'd try out the daily pages. At first it was so hard to think of enough stuff to fill three whole pages, but after a few weeks I started to look forward to my early-morning coffee and that time alone, just thinking. Now I think I might want to join some kind of club—a book club maybe, or find friends who like going to movies. I know for sure I'm interested in exploring my creative side again."

THE IMPORTANCE OF THE HERE AND NOW

From Perpetual Preoccupation to Appreciating the Moment

You're in the kitchen. The TV is blaring, and you're preparing dinner. Tonight you thought you'd make something that didn't come from a can, so you're chopping vegetables. You're thinking about the proposal that's due at work, or you're worrying about the next credit card bill. Or maybe you're chewing over a fight you had with your sister, carrying the disappointment and anger in the muscles of your shoulders. You cut your finger. You keep going. The evening news in the background is depressing. You sit down at the computer to check on the weather for tomorrow. Will the kids need their raincoats and boots?

"Mom?" Your daughter calls out from across the room. "Mom?"

"Mmmm . . . just a minute," you answer, staring at the weather map.

"Mom, today I—"

Is that storm cloud on the screen moving toward your neighborhood or away? "OK, hon, hang on just a sec."

"Ugh, never mind!" Footsteps. A door shuts.

"Honey, what is it?" You turn around, but she's already left.

And there you are. That moment, that opportunity, is gone in one fell swoop.

> *The foolish man seeks happiness in the distance,*
> *the wise grows it under his feet.*
> —James Oppenheim, poet

We're all busy doing many things at the same time—it's just the way our life is nowadays. Right? But do you ever get the sense that while you're so busy juggling your responsibilities, you're missing out on really connecting with your kids? Here's an interesting fact: we all feel it's because we have *less* time now, but statistics show we actually spend *more* time with our kids than our mothers spent with us. In 1965, mothers spent an average of ten hours a week focused on their children, whereas now they spend fourteen hours a week with them, according to Suzanne M. Bianchi, chair of the Department of Sociology at the University of Maryland. "It's almost like it doesn't matter how much they do, they feel they never do enough," Bianchi said of modern mothers in her 2006 book, *Changing Rhythms of American Family Life.*

So why the difference between perception and reality? Truth is, the time we do spend with our families just isn't registering with us or with them. How often are you with your children, giving them your undivided attention? You may be in their presence—in the home or in the car—or doing things for them, but are you really *with* them? Ironically, having a mental time-out can actually help us engage more fully with the activity we're undertaking: here a time-out means allowing yourself a pause, an interruption, in the flow of activity so we can *focus* our thoughts and *regroup.*

Here we tackle the idea of living in the moment, not for yesterday or tomorrow, but for right now. Some people call it mindfulness, others call it being present (some may call it BS, but read on). Do you:

- ► Dream constantly about the future, but find it hard to enjoy the day-to-day?
- ► Dwell in the past, musing over the good old days?
- ► Rush through fun activities, so you can get to the work or chores that need to be done?
- ► Wake at night thinking about your to-do list?
- ► Have a tight chest during everyday activities?
- ► Experience sorrow or regret from which it's impossible to move on?
- ► Find it hard to forgive and forget?

These are symptoms of what the Buddhists call the "monkey mind," when we're unable to keep our pesky minds still. "Most of the day is hectic. Even when the kids are gone, there's always something brewing," said Serena, a mom from New York who has two high schoolers. Our culture values industry and progress—and with that comes not only constant action, but also anxiety.

> The secret of health for the mind and the body is not to mourn for the past, not to worry about the future, nor to anticipate troubles, but to live in the present moment wisely and earnestly.
> —Dalai Lama, Tibetan Buddhist leader

On top of that, many of us live with violence, hardship, tragedy, financial stress, or natural and man-made disasters, and often our reaction to these challenges is to try to tighten our grip. But *that* sure backfires—it can turn us into hovering mothers who hyperparent our children, something we swore we'd never do! Mothers brood and worry instead of being able to experience the simple joy of being.

Being Fully *Present*? But I'm Right Here . . .

The three of us are convinced that the ability to be fully present is one of the most important secrets to enjoying the process of mothering; we've heard this theme echoed in so many mothers' stories. Buddhism teaches that you can achieve discernment, wisdom, insight, and enlightenment by becoming more aware of your body, mind, and feelings. Western religions, such as Catholicism or Protestantism, encourage churchgoing and prayer as a way to pause in a restless world. Within the Jewish religion, Shabbat is practiced, which can be translated as "to cease" or "to sit:" a weekly commitment to stop work and unnecessary activity for twenty-four hours. Muslims perform *Salah*, which is praying to Mecca five times a day to encourage consistent mindfulness. By concentrating through meditation, prayer, silence, and close focus on the task at hand, you can achieve a state of rest right where you are. In your day-to-day life, this can translate into finding real satisfaction in an hour of building a puzzle with your child, instead of being antsy and preoccupied.

> *The really happy person is one who can enjoy the scenery when on a detour.*
> **—Anonymous**

In learning to work through initial feelings of boredom or distractibility, we can recognize those seemingly empty moments as an opportunity to let the imagination fly or give the mind permission to rest. Here's the real clincher: unless we model this respect for the moment, *this* moment, to our children, what kind of adults will they become? Gillian, mother of three from Arizona, complained she couldn't sit still for even

KATRIN DRAGS HERSELF TO THE PARK

A few years ago, we were visiting my parents in London during spring break. I had all sorts of plans: I wanted to show my kids all the places I'd loved when I was growing up and take them to the best museums and galleries. It was going to be great.

Well, the first day no one but me woke up 'til 11:30 È È I was so restless, I'd already been out to get coffee and a paper, walked along the High Street for an hour, and then sat around for a couple *more* hours fuming about how we were wasting precious time. Six days in London out of a whole year, and they were going to spend it sleeping? But I knew better than to rouse them. My kids are not early risers. I used to see that as an unexpected bonus, but as they got older I was starting to find it frustrating.

Finally the three of them emerged, puffy-eyed and grumpy. I tried to hurry them along, but Svenja, who was five, started crying. When I proposed going to the Tate Gallery or the British Museum, Peter, who was almost eleven, began to pout. He was too tired to go to a museum, he complained. Couldn't we do something fun?

"The daffodils are out in Hyde Park," my mother said. "The kids'll love it."

That wasn't exactly my idea of something enriching, but I decided, what the hell, we had five more days to go, we could make up for lost time tomorrow.

As I tromped through the park, I watched the three kids running after the Canadian geese. Frankly, I was pretty irritable. Then Peter came up to me and slipped his hand in mine. I don't know exactly what it was about that moment, but a realization hit me like a plank of wood in the face: my kids were having a blast in a place I loved. I studied Peter for a minute. He wasn't a surly teenager yet, but I knew I'd have my comeuppance one day soon enough—if my own appalling teenage behavior was anything to go by. And here he was, *holding my hand.* An image of him as a grown man flit through my mind. How much longer would he willingly, unself-consciously, hold my hand?

That very day I understood how fleeting my time with my children would be. I grasped his hand a little harder and slowed down the pace. It was the best, most rewarding vacation I've ever had because it taught me to really pay attention to the little things. I've carried that appreciation with me to this day, no matter how many more important things there are on my agenda.

five minutes with her kids, because she was always so preoccu-pied thinking about work, dinner, or chores. Slowing down and really being present with our children models for them what it means to have a true connection with others. Isn't that ulti-mately what we all yearn for?

Living mindfully is the very opposite of multitasking. In a 2006 article in *Neuron*, René Marois, a neuroscientist and director of the Human Information Processing Laboratory at Vanderbilt University said, "The human brain, with its hun-dred billion neurons and hundreds of trillions of synaptic connections, is an amazing cognitive powerhouse, but a core limitation is an inability to concentrate on two things at once." Through functional magnetic resonance imaging, Dr. Marois conducted a study proving that people completed assignments more effectively—more quickly and with fewer errors—when concentrating on a single task at a time rather than spreading themselves thin.

Mindfulness is the aware, balanced acceptance of the present experience. It isn't more complicated than that. It is opening to or receiving the present moment, pleasant or unpleasant, just as it is, without either clinging to it or rejecting it.
—Sylvia Boorstein, teacher

Ironically, in our modern culture, women see multitasking as positive; in school, during their careers, and as parents, they are constantly expected to juggle many balls in the air all at

---

FROM PROBLEM TO SOLUTION

Jane, Mother of Three from Ohio

Jane is in the car a lot. Usually when she's at home, she likes things peaceful: no music, no TV, no shouting. But when she's in the car, she's trapped. In the backseat, her three kids bicker endlessly. They're not really fighting, they're just jumpy: playing, pulling, asking, denying, calling out, laughing. "It drove me *so* nuts," Jane said, "and I just couldn't get them to be quiet." So what did she do? She made a few CDs of her "soft music" playlist. When things get too rowdy, she slips it in and turns up the volume. It helps focus the kids' attention and create a sense of calm.

---

once. Let's be honest, how often have you moaned about men being incapable of multitasking? We sure have!

One Thing at a Time

In this day and age, there's really no way around having to do many things at once. But the key to being able to fully enjoy our lives—as they are *right now*—is to find greater clarity of purpose: to be selfish enough so we are able to determine our priorities and then to live by them.

When your mind is racing, it's hard to savor anything, let alone simple pleasures like a child's smile. How often have you caught yourself in these situations?

▸ You're on the phone and one of your kids is trying to tell you something, but you're not listening.

▸ A child is leisurely recounting a story, and you're thinking: Hurry up, we'll be late!

▸ A list of to-dos is streaming through your mind the entire time you're doing an activity that's supposed to be fun.

> *Yesterday is wood, tomorrow is ashes.*
> *Only today does the fire burn brightly.*
> —Inuit saying

When everyone's bickering, your husband's late, or you're looking for the ponytail holders, the house is chaotic, and you're angry, it's good to stop for a moment. Just take a time-out. Check in with your mind: it's probably whirling. When your head is spinning, it's almost impossible to be in control. You might find that after taking a few deep breaths and stopping all movement you're able to approach whatever situation you're in with greater composure. Joanna, single mom of two from New Mexico, said she practices this every time things get hectic, and it helps her move from irritation to gratitude. "I can take in the energy and life swirling around me," she explained, "and feel happy to not be alone, rather than get mad at the turmoil."

It's a modern malady to be addicted to conveniences like the BlackBerry, cell phones, or the computer. In addition, background music is often on or the TV is blaring, and you just steadily plow through it all, barely noticing. Older kids are even more extreme: they IM while listening to music, while researching a paper, while talking to their parents! But in a 2007 *New York Times* article, David E. Meyer, director of the Brain, Cognition, and Action Lab at the University of Michigan, says all this activity can have serious negative implications: "People lose the skill and the will to maintain concentration, and they get mental antsyness."

There's also another problem. All this multitasking and juggling affects our kids. They're watching us; they emulate what they see. Colleen, high school teacher and mother of three from Maryland, says kids nowadays are so busy and spend so much time socializing on the computer instead of hanging out face-to-face that they find interpersonal relationships hard. "I see these kids in school who barely know how to have a real conversation anymore," she said. Children under eighteen years old spend an average of more than ninety minutes a day on the computer, according to a 2005 Kaiser Family Foundation study, and 75 percent of that time is spent instant messaging, reading, or writing e-mails.

So what's the solution? Mothers need to model what it's like to really pay attention to someone by looking people in the eyes, listening, and absorbing what the other person is saying. If mothers slow down a bit, concentrating on doing one thing at a time and doing it well, they'll teach their children by example how to plug into the moment and live more consciously.

FROM PROBLEM TO SOLUTION

Katie, Mother of Five from Maine

When Katie was recovering from breast cancer, she had to be on bed rest for two months. Amazingly, she came away from the experience feeling as though her life had been enriched. That quiet time helped her see through the chaotic rhythm of her family's schedule and realize she wanted to just hang out more. "It was like torture at first," she said. "Then I came to love the peace, the incredible peace, of being still."

How Time Flies

Oftentimes you achieve clarity about your priorities only by experiencing what you *don't* like. Being frenzied always feels bad. But you don't always recognize how stressful it is to live constantly on the go, whether mentally or physically. Having a loved one get sick, falling ill ourselves, helping a child with a disability, being forced to move due to a job transfer—from our focus groups we learned that it often takes these kinds of challenges to jerk mothers into a whole new awareness.

Wouldn't it be wonderful if it didn't take a tragedy to shake us out of our robotic busyness? By enjoying the process of life—the day-to-day stuff, not just the end goal—we'll get the most out of our limited time here on Earth. By freeing up our minds to focus on one thing at a time, rather than swinging from thought to thought like a restless monkey, we also open ourselves up to curiosity.

Ah, remember how open and curious we were as kids? With genuine curiosity comes a deeper connection to our world and the childlike ability to be fully present in the moment.

ANNE'S EXPEDITIONS TO ~~MOUNT KILIMANJARO~~ THE GROCERY STORE

When my twins were babies, it took every ounce of physical and emotional energy to get them out the door and to the grocery store. Just thinking about it transports me right back to those incredibly demanding and exhausting years. I would have to really muster up the energy to prepare for our big outing of the day: food shopping.

Already feeling frazzled, I'd arrive at the market, grab the car door handle with my one free pinky finger, prop open the door with one of my feet, and suddenly I'd catch a glimpse of myself in the window. Unbrushed hair framing the baby spit-up on both shoulders of my sweater. What a sight! Hopefully, nobody would notice me.

But inevitably, as I lugged two car seats around, an older woman would approach me and say something like, "Ah! Twins! What *special* days! Don't you go wishing them away!" An aisle or so later, another mother would crow, "Enjoy it, darling. It goes so quickly!" And minutes later, I'd be stopped by yet another woman who'd comment on how lucky I was.

Lucky? Truthfully, I felt anything but lucky.

Yet these older women clearly knew something that I didn't. It was a consistent theme: enjoy it now, it goes by so fast. When life feels out of control, it's easy to lose sight of how special the moment is. But they had already learned that when children are grown and gone, those feelings of doubt we experience fade to nothing in our memories. I did have to power through the early years with all the energy and commitment I could muster, but those comments stuck with me. I eventually got to the point where I could actually enjoy my girls and even consider having *another* baby: my little powerhouse, Jay.

Now when I'm in a grocery store—I can hardly believe it!—I find myself commenting on adorable babies and yearning for the early years. Seeing mothers doting over their tiny children always gives me renewed appreciation for the struggles and joys of motherhood. I know that everything I'm living through now will be just another distant memory one day, so I'm mindful of trying to fully live every minute.

An Invitation to Introspection

One result of stripping away the layers of learned behavior that cause snap reactions and focusing on the now is that we become much more self-aware. We learn what our trigger points are and how to redirect our minds so that we don't dwell on unproductive thoughts, such as minor resentments or pining for a rosy but distant future. And observing ourselves and our kids with greater concentration and compassion can lead to a stunning thing: the recognition of what our kids can teach *us*!

There's nothing like a child to force you to look long and hard at yourself in the mirror. If you haven't experienced this moment as a mother, you will soon: your child comes out with a statement, or reacts to a situation, or moves in such a way that you *see yourself*. No doubt about it, that child is a product of you, your parenting, and your personality.

> *Yesterday's the past and tomorrow's the future.*
> *Today is a gift—which is why they call it the present.*
> **Bil Keane, cartoonist**

Our children teach us more about ourselves than we could ever learn alone in a lifetime. They will challenge everything we thought we knew about ourselves, our partners, or life in general. Sometimes we succeed in being a patient, resourceful, and consistent teacher to our children, and sometimes we fail. It's through the good times and the not-so-good times that the best and the worst about us will be revealed. Our children love us for all that we are: the good, the not so good, and the ugly.

Through our children we will also reexperience things that have been long buried. This revelation can have a variety of unexpected consequences and joys. Being active in their schooling

SUSAN TRIES TO REINVENT HER PAST

Cole's big ballet recital was just days away. For the final rehearsal, Cole and I spent hours getting the costume to hang just right, organizing the straps like an intricate puzzle, and using an entire bottle of hair spray to create the perfect bun. Once at the hall, we waited for hours with the other cute ballerinas and then, finally, the teacher called our group and all the girls jumped up to the stage.

But Cole, in her big butterfly costume, was superglued to my lap. She would not budge. It was all I could do not to force her up there. I wanted her to experience what I had experienced. I wanted her to be on that stage. I nudged a little and then realized this wasn't happening today. I'd just have to wait until the show tomorrow to see my ballerina performing.

So the next day, we went through all of the same activities: hair, makeup, and dress. With excitement building, Cole's group was called to the stage to perform in front of the crowd.

But Cole clung to me.

She had promised she was going up on that stage! I wanted that so badly for her. But it was not to be, at least not that year.

Year two, Cole was all revved-up for the recital. She learned her dance cold and was one of the leaders of the group. I thought: How great for her. She'll never forget the wonderful feeling of being onstage. But at the recital, she only had to glance up at me and I knew that she was going to watch all her friends go onstage, from the vantage point of my lap, and that she'd enjoy every minute of it.

It hit me that Cole was becoming her own person; she was going to be the keeper of her stage career. Actually, I think she was quite pleased with her situation. I realized that she was not me and she was not performing for me.

Cole has now gone on to dance in front of an audience many times, and she does love it, but it doesn't really matter whether she gets onstage or not. For both of us, the experience of going together to class every week for years—enjoying each other's company—is the real gift we're getting and giving each other.

refreshes our own minds to the endless variety and depth of life: we may have forgotten all about the Battle of Bunker Hill or the excitement we felt when we first read the poetry of John Donne, or we may have suppressed the anxiety of gym class as a six-year-old or sitting for the SAT as a teen. Some aspects of our childhood may have been painful for us—bullying, failing, difficulty with our parents—and we're bound to relive some of those traumas and joys through our own children.

FROM PROBLEM TO SOLUTION

Jennifer, Mother of Two from Pennsylvania

Jennifer has two girls: Sue loves theater and Claudia plays lacrosse. During their rehearsals and practices, Jennifer used to while away the time chatting or reading a magazine. Then one day at Sue's play rehearsal, she recognized herself in her child's self-conscious grandstanding. "I thought, oh my god, that's me!" said Jennifer. "I began thinking about my own behavior: how I like to be the center of attention, and whether that's always so good." Later, when her other daughter, Claudia, was at a lacrosse practice, Jennifer saw a reflection of her own competitiveness and limitless energy in Claudia's playing style. "By paying more attention to details, not always being so distracted, you know, I feel like I'm learning so much about my own personality, as well as theirs," Jennifer said. "It's so unexpected, but great!"

We're also challenged by our kids to rethink positions or character traits we may have taken for granted. Paying attention to what pushes our buttons can help us understand where *we* need to grow and change.

Practicing Peacefulness

Meditation can provide the key to plugging into the moment by teaching us how to banish those frisky monkey thoughts that can cause us so much anguish. When the mind is calm, the body and spirit can connect to the present without interference, judgment, or fear. The primary goal of meditating is to guide the mind to a still place, and to achieve this, we have to give it something else to focus on. Though in practice this can be incredibly hard to do, practitioners swear by it. In *O, The Oprah Magazine*'s January 2003 issue, Dr. Mehmet Oz, director of the Cardiovascular Institute at Columbia University Medical Center, says that meditating "lowers blood pressure and heart rate and counteracts secretion of stress hormones like cortisol." Sounds good, don't you think?

It's all about uncoupling sensations in your body from the thoughts about them. You're giving your whirling mind a much-needed time-out. There are loads of benefits, such as:

▶ Reduction of anxiety or even depression (which also helps you sleep better)
▶ Learning to let go, which prevents stress from building and becoming cumulative; no more pounding heart and racing thoughts
▶ Deep relaxation during waking hours, which increases your energy level and productivity, as well as improving concentration and memory
▶ Calming your mind to reduce—or even prevent— some psychosomatic disorders such as hypertension, migraines, headaches, asthma, and ulcers
▶ Reducing chronic pain

If your mind is empty, it is always ready for anything; it is open to everything. In the beginner's mind there are many possibilities, but in the expert's there are few.
—Shunryu Suzuki, Zen priest

According to a 2003 *Time* magazine article, ten million Americans say they practice some form of meditation regularly—that's twice as many as a decade earlier. You can do it too, right now! If you have ten minutes, here's one way to start what we learned from a physical therapist:

1. Sit comfortably in an upright chair. Close your eyes and begin to focus on your breath. With your mouth closed in a slight smile, inhale and exhale through your nose.
2. Begin to notice where the inhalation ends and the exhalation begins, and vice versa.
3. Focus on the pause between the breaths. Notice the pause becoming longer and the breaths as well. Find comfort and relaxation in your breath and how deeply peaceful the present moment is.
4. Practice this for five to ten minutes. When a thought enters your mind, imagine putting it in a drawer and closing it.
5. End with a positive thought: with each inhalation, acknowledge a blessing in your life and with the exhalation, give that blessing more energy or gratitude.

FROM PROBLEM TO SOLUTION

Sasha, Mother of Three from New Zealand

Sasha's first child, Sam, developed lymphoma when he was a year old. Over the next five years, Sam underwent constant surgeries and treatments. Sasha quit work to focus on him and then had two more babies. At times she didn't know how she'd get through it all, it was so harrowing. Then she discovered the healing power of meditation. "My mantra is said over and over while taking deep breaths—it helps me to fall asleep or to focus during the day," she explained. Here it is: she says "Life in" while breathing in, "Love out" while breathing out. She pauses and reverses it: "Love in" while breathing in, "Life out" while breathing out. "It sounds pretty simple, but it helps to breathe in the good and breathe out the bad. It's enabled me to realize what is important and what is not."

6. Take note: there's no right way to meditate! Just give it a go and accept that whatever steps you're taking are better than not trying at all.

The Meditation Society of America currently has 108 meditation practices listed on its website (including guided imagery, chanting, and listening to music or prayers), so there's no shortage of techniques to try! Remember the following three things, and you'll be on your way to finding more to enjoy in the everyday process of being a mother:

- ▸ **Notice:** Look and see.
- ▸ **Accept:** Let it be.
- ▸ **Let go:** Be free.

> The present is never our goal: the past and the present are our means, the future is our goal. Thus we never live but we hope to live, and in always hoping to be happy, it is inevitable that we will never be so.
> —Blaise Pascal, mathematician

OK—What About When Living in the Moment Sucks?

Frankly, everyone has moments when they can't enjoy their kids or husbands and when the here and now just sucks. It doesn't have to be because of some big calamity—it can be something as simple as having to suffer through a child's tantrum in a public place or listening to your kids fight while you're trying to enjoy a nature walk. Jean from Virginia, mother of two, said she can feel the waves of irritation and then anger wash over her and become all-consuming when the moment becomes chaotic. Learning how to deflect automatic responses like this by taking your own time-out is crucial and can often avert a disastrous parental meltdown!

FROM PROBLEM TO SOLUTION

Barbara, Mother of Four from Texas

Often when Barbara is preparing dinner, her kids are hungry and tired and start to bicker. They like to do their homework at the kitchen table, but by 6:30 ιɛ̀ Ὲ they've had it with the togetherness. "I'm usually so quiet and patient," Barbara said. "And then I just blow! I feel so bad afterward, but I really can't help myself." It was such a regular and demoralizing occurrence that she decided to do something about it. She taped a happy picture of each of her kids when they were tiny onto her kitchen cupboards. Now when the fighting starts, she'll glance at their smiling faces and she finds that she loses her cool a lot less often.

From our discussions with women, here are the top three ways to come to a deep understanding of yourself and your reactions, so you can avoid letting one bad moment ruin your day:

1. Know yourself. Pay attention to timing. If you're often wiped out at the end of the day, make sure to keep things calm by not piling too much on your plate. Or if one particular thing a child does always gets your goat, examine how you can learn to accept it or change it, and reflect on whether your child could be mirroring an aspect of your *own* behavior that you don't like.

2. Reorient your mind. Practice ways to take your mind off the moment so that you can reenter the situation with greater composure. Moms who meditate or do yoga often say they're able to tap into a feeling of serenity at stressful moments without even trying that hard. It's a matter of conditioning your mind to respond to certain calming activities, like breathing exercises or visualization.

3. Control your attitude. Make a conscious decision to operate with a more positive attitude. This can be learned. Sometimes it's a matter of turning something mundane, such as chopping vegetables or filing paperwork, into something therapeutic. You know how some monotonous activities, like running, can be comforting?

Henrietta, mother of two from Florida, has a slide show that constantly runs on her computer. Every time she walks past it, she sees another memory flicker by. "There's Jack eating sand one second, and the next he's finishing up fourth grade," she says. "I never thought it would all rush by like this!" Living in the here and now is ultimately about learning to appreciate the life we are living right at this present moment. It brings out the best in us and allows us to focus on the good things that are already a part of our everyday lives.

TIPS FROM THE TRENCHES

▶ **Get on your knees.** Too often a child wants to talk to us and our minds are elsewhere. Sometimes we miss a tiny opportunity to connect with our children that would be much more meaningful than the hours we spend ferrying them around. Next time your kid wants to tell you something, get down on your knees. Looking into his or her eyes helps you really listen to what your child is trying to share.

▶ **Recognize the value of boredom.** When you catch yourself feeling bored—for example, if you're at a kid's after-school game—try to relax *into* the boredom. Focus on the dynamics of the team, study the faces and bodies of the kids, and find pleasure in the fleeting moment. Pay attention to your thoughts slowing down, your body relaxing, and your appreciation of the small things of beauty around you. We can also teach our kids so much by letting them grapple with boredom—they'll become much more self-sufficient and imaginative. Another way to look at being bored is to see it as an opportunity to let go of our constant striving and find solace in the simple rhythms of life.

▶ **Discover the joy of sharing an interest with your kids.** Many women told us what a thrilling discovery it was once they began to share interests with their children. Tapping into old passions—those hobbies we neglected while building our careers, the pastimes or sports we used to enjoy when we had freer lives—and reliving them again through our children can be incredibly rewarding. Were you a gymnast, a reader of fantasy novels, a swimmer, or a chess player? Did you love old movies or dance music? But be careful not to push your kids too hard: just introduce them to the things you love and see what happens.

▶ **Advertise loudly and often.** Make sure to point out —to yourself, the children, and your spouse—the good things that are happening *when* they happen. Say, "Isn't this great! We're here together, hanging out!" or "Hey, we managed to all sit down for a family dinner," or "It's so special to lie here with you, reading this funny little story together."

▶ **Engage in forced relaxation.** There are many moments when your body tenses up and you don't even realize it. We store that tension for the rest of the day, and it seeps into our thoughts and actions. Next time you're driving, consciously relax your shoulders. Move them up and down, and make sure they're not up to your chin! Loosen your grip on the steering wheel. Squint your eyes once or twice, do a couple of big fake smiles to help your face muscles relax. Try that when you're doing anything on autopilot.

▶ **Learn to compartmentalize.** When we set our minds to something, it's amazing what we can do. By practicing the art of compartmentalizing our thoughts, we can learn to focus more effectively on the moment. For instance, when you're at work and you're thinking of your family, shift your mind back to the matter at hand. One way to do this is to imagine putting the thought into a car and watching it drive off. When you're with the kids, be aware of your thoughts so that you can banish work concerns from your mind. When you're aware of where your head is at, you can steer it back on track if you need to.

► **Take note of nature.** Nature has a way of opening our eyes to the miraculous. Remark on one thing in nature every single day, whether it's the new buds on the trees, the wisps of cloud streaking through the sky, or the reflection of your face in a puddle or a lake. Even when we're surrounded by despair or plagued by irritations, there is always beauty to be found in the natural world.

► **Connect with a higher power.** Even if you're not religious, try a soothing ritual such as praying every day, holding hands before a family dinner, going to church or synagogue or mosque once a week, or repeating a mantra to yourself such as "Let it go." Giving ourselves up to fate may seem defeatist to some, but to others it's the key to accepting the challenges we face. So many women have told us it's easier to let go of sorrow or disappointment and enjoy the small, everyday moments of grace when they acknowledge a higher power.

► **Get your hands dirty.** When your children are doing a project, get right in there and do it with them. Or do your own! Get your hands dirty painting rocks. Smush some clay. Write your own little story. Draw a picture with charcoal. Sometimes it's incredibly freeing to let ourselves be children again and not be concerned about how beautifully we sculpt a piece of art or how successfully we can draw a still life. Do it just for fun.

► **Reactivate your curiosity.** There's something so energizing and positive about being curious. Next time someone tells you a story, don't just listen but ask questions. And then ask some more. Train your mind to be open again, to absorb and desire information. If you learn something interesting one day, do some research and find out more about it. Always wondered what it was like inside a factory, or in an artist's studio, or on a boat? Find a way to experience things you were curious about as a child.

I TRIED THE TIPS! NADIA, MOTHER OF TWO FROM MASSACHUSETTS

"I don't usually spend a lot of time outside. I live in the city and there's no green space near us. So this seemed like a real challenge for me, to focus more on nature. One night, I just turned my head and there it was, this incredible sunset. I pointed it out to my daughter, Lulu. Then I started noticing birds—not pigeons, but real birds—and some bluebells in a flowerpot on a fire escape. A few days ago, Lulu tugged on my sleeve and pointed out the colors of the setting sun! It was really neat to see my appreciation filter through to her."

THE VALUE OF DOWNTIME

From Living in Perpetual Motion to Hearing Your Own Voice in the Silence

Does your day sound anything like this? Up at the crack of dawn, Diane starts the coffeemaker, unloads the dishwasher, sits down to write the to-do list for the day. "Don't forget to bring the permission slip for the field trip!" she calls out to her son, buttering toast with one hand and pouring a big cup of coffee with the other, "and take your basketball shirt, it's game day." She runs to the basement to grab socks out of the dryer, a pair of mittens that were left on the stairs, and a child's backpack . . . shoot, it's almost time to get the kids to the bus stop!

> *Restlessness and discontent are the first necessities of progress.*
> —Thomas A. Edison, inventor

The phone rings, but she can't reach it fast enough. Move quickly, she thinks, it's almost time to go. As she grabs sticky plates, she clasps the phone to one ear to check messages. Then, it's off: kids to the bus stop, her three-year-old to day care, and Diane to work. During her lunch break, she's at the bookstore looking up how to deal with a parent who has Alzheimer's disease. On the way home, she stops by the grocery store and dashes through the aisles. In her mind the mental list of to-dos runs like a never-ending tape: Don't forget to pay the bill for the piano lessons. Call Dad back when I get home. Pick up my new glasses.

Once the kids are back from day care, play dates, or sports, Diane monitors homework, slaps food on the table, and returns phone calls. Tantrums and dramas come and go. Her nerves are frayed. Her husband's running late. Bill-paying will have to wait till tomorrow, even though they'll end up owing interest—there's just no time.

In this day, there hasn't been a single free moment for reflection or uninterrupted thoughts. The pace is relentless, and it always is! Like many mothers, Diane is yawning well before her kids are ready for bed. The tedium and predictability of these rituals gives her a slight, buzzing headache. Diane realizes that she's forgotten to eat anything other than leftover waffles and broken Oreos all day. Oh, and she picked at the chicken nuggets. Another mental note to self: cook healthier food.

When she wakes up at 2:37 A.M., her head starts spinning again. No juice boxes for the lunches, forgot to call Dad, and need to make those plans for Matty's party. Another endless day looms ahead of her. She wonders when they can swing taking that long-awaited vacation.

This woman badly needs a break.

Another mom, Abigail, follows much the same pattern: up early doing chores, with things forgotten, overlooked, and crammed in. Of course she's running late. But when her toddler spills his juice, she slows down before swooping in to wipe it up—she's caught sight of the expression on his face and he looks so mortified that she laughs. She's throwing together a packed lunch (there's no more peanut butter) and calling her spouse at the office (to remind him today's his day to pick up the dry cleaning) when the bus pulls up. Kids run to the door, books flying, hair uncombed. A few minutes later, Abigail's friend toots her horn out front: she's doing the run to day care this week.

> The quieter you become, the more you are able to hear.
> —Zen saying

Her watch tells her she has some time before her train leaves. She can either clean up the kitchen or see her plan through. This morning when she woke up, she decided to walk to the station instead of driving. As the weather becomes more agreeable, this is her daily routine. The idea of fifteen minutes of cool, fresh air—of enjoying the sound of her heels clacking rhythmically on the pavement—makes all her earlier activities seem less of a drag.

About five minutes into her walk, the narrow muscles that run across the middle of Abigail's back (often so painfully tight) have softened. Perhaps she hears a long, sweet note of music from an open window or a resounding silence that allows her to pay attention to filling her lungs with deep breaths of air, feeding her muscles with oxygen.

As she nears the station, the memory of something wonderful is lurking in the tranquil recesses of her mind: a flower by the roadside, a bold pattern she caught a glimpse of yesterday, the blue sky against a wind-whipped ocean. She gives the image time to form and then lets it go. No mental debris is cluttering up her mind—no to-do lists, no frantic recollections of chores forgotten, no demons whispering that this mom is just being lazy.

At work her pace never lets up; during her lunch break, she gets Henry's shoes fixed and picks up her prescriptions. But she enjoys the walk through the city and hears the same comforting click-clack of shoes that she heard this morning. Abigail knows that she'll have fifteen minutes to herself once she gets off that train and heads home again.

This woman has had downtime.

She tries to consistently give herself mental time-outs, so she can feel more grounded and bring more positive energy to her day's responsibilities.

Just Take Five!

The reality of our lives as mothers—whether we stay at home or go to work, have one kid or five, are old pros at child rearing or new to the game—is that we've all experienced the daily frustrations of not having enough time to do things properly, of being stretched so thin that we snap and complain. Sometimes we'll go for days, weeks, months—even *years* in some cases—operating this way, wondering why we feel so little joy in our lives.

Many of us have to be pushed to the limits of our health and happiness before we understand that downtime isn't a luxury we need once in a blue moon, but a frequent necessity.

So What Exactly Does *Downtime* Mean?

Downtime is a perk—or so most people think. It's just not something a busy mother, whether working outside the home or in, feels she has a right to. If you're like most of the moms we've talked to, *downtime* means this: feeling guilty for taking time off. (*Guilt* is a word we'd like to banish from our vocabularies, but more on that later.) As soon as we take a little downtime for ourselves, we feel as though we're doing something naughty, like skipping school.

> Happiness is not a station you arrive at,
> but a manner of traveling.
> —Margaret Lee Runbeck, writer

Anyway, that's all beside the point because we just don't have time for it, do we? We're much too busy to be standing still. Everyone wants something from us, and between chores,

ANNE GETS A WAKE-UP CALL

I was sitting in my car on the way to picking up my four-year-old from a friend's house when I spotted red brake lights in the distance: cars stopped on the road. I checked the clock and calculated that I'd be ten, maybe fifteen, minutes late to pick Jay up. My cell phone was at home, out of juice. I still had on my work clothes, and I hadn't showered that morning, as I'd overslept. Though I had had a low-grade headache all day, I hadn't come anywhere near drinking my eight glasses of water. My mouth was parched.

A few months earlier I'd gone back to work. But I made one big mistake: I kept up my busy schedule, confident that I could pack it all in. That day on the road, seeing the red lights ahead of me triggered something. My heart started to race, my vision blurred, and I felt weak. Images of crashing the car or fainting at the wheel flitted through my mind, so I pulled over onto the grass embankment.

I was experiencing overwhelming anxiety. I understood I had to make some fundamental changes in my life.

It was pretty simple: I was trying to fit too much in. I hadn't seen how much harm it was doing to me and to my family, too. The pace of life I was setting didn't allow enough time to simply be with my kids.

One Sunday, shortly after experiencing that same anxiety again, I was sitting in church with my eyes shut, the kids squirming next to me. I began to concentrate on my breathing . . . in . . . out . . . in . . . out. I became aware that I was feeling calm and peaceful. I stopped and listened to my breathing again.

When I got home from church, I found that I really didn't want to tackle any to-do list, I just wanted to be with the kids and Bruce. I went out to the yard and sat on the stone wall. For about twenty minutes I just watched the kids jumping on the trampoline. I went in to tidy up the kitchen a bit and found myself moving more slowly. I actually began to enjoy the process—and the time in my house.

I decided that on my commute to and from work I would try to find the same sense of peace. I put down the BlackBerry, turned off the phone, and packed away the daily planner. I found a seat on the train and started to breathe . . . in . . . out . . . in . . . out. There it was again, that feeling of inner calm. I thought to myself, "If I had ever known how good this felt, I would have started earlier in motherhood!"

work, food, and driving, there's just not a spare minute to lavish on ourselves.

Often we snatch downtime secretively. We've zoned out in front of the television for a minute, and we know we should get up and put away the dishes, make those appointments, or actu-

FROM PROBLEM TO SOLUTION

Deidre, Mother of Three from Illinois

Deidre works the early shift in a family-run business and has an hour to herself before her children get off the bus after school. She clears away crusty breakfast dishes, makes beds, and starts in on the laundry. Come 3 ʁ ʁ she's already pretty cranky. So she tried an experiment: instead of filling this time alone with chores, she makes a cup of tea and watches her favorite TV show that she's recorded from the evening before. "It's not that long, but I really feel I'm relaxing," she said. "When the kids get home, I've got renewed patience." Now she tidies things up when the children are back. Deidre has even managed to get them in the habit of making their own beds and bringing down the laundry hamper.

ally read the newspaper instead of just throwing it away, but we can't seem to move. Yoga makes us feel peaceful, but it takes too darn long. In the evenings when the kids are sleeping, a beer or a drink often makes up for the lack of calm we've had during the day. We find temporary solutions that aren't really solutions at all, but only duct tape on a broken pipe.

So what do we really mean when we say *downtime*? We're not talking about those rushed moments, crammed in between the stuff of our lives. We're suggesting you actually give yourself a time-out—from ten minutes, to an hour, to a day—when:

- ► You choose what to do with your time. You're doing something you *want* to do, not what someone else *expects* you to do.
- ► You've temporarily escaped from your roles as mother, spouse, or professional and are simply being yourself.
- ► You have given yourself permission to do nothing: you are *being*, not *doing*.
- ► You're allowing your body and mind to relax.

One important thing we discovered on our journey as friends and mothers in the age of doing too much is that downtime means totally different things to different women. Because she's so busy, Anne finds her daily quiet time right in the midst of the hustle and bustle of life. Susan sees her car as a refuge and often gets places early so she can sit and listen to the radio in peace. Katrin seeks creative outlets so she can continue to find pleasure in her work and home life.

Silencing the Inner (and Outer) Critics

The three of us know from our own experiences that taking time-outs from parenting is a necessity. But truth be told, even though the majority of women in our focus groups recognized how much they needed a break, they rarely took one. After all,

KATRIN'S SKIRMISH WITH THE KILLER MOSQUITOES

I'd just completed my first novel and was stumped for ideas on the next book. Since I was new in town, I didn't know a single writer or artist in my area. Writing was turning out to be really lonely work.

In the meantime, I'd just had my third child, Svenja, a sweet little thing who caused me no trouble but turned my three-year-old, Greta, into a possessed child: talking to me constantly, cutting her own hair, drawing on walls, destroying my things.

One night at the dinner table, Greta was screeching away at me. Distracted by clearing the dishes, I had pretty much blocked her out, and she didn't like that. She took her plate of food and dropped it on the floor.

That got my attention.

I had two choices: I could smack her, or I could run away. I chose the latter. I raced out the back door and into the woods. The mosquitoes were like Harrier jets. Crouching in the bushes, I looked through the kitchen window. Greta's voice was the only sound that I could hear (other than the droning of bloodsuckers).

This was a real low point for me. I felt that I was failing as a mother, and the sense of accomplishment I usually got from my work had vanished.

That weekend, my brother-in-law gave me a lot of his old stuff from art school, among it pieces of glass, lead, cutting tools, and a soldering iron. I cleared a small table for myself in the basement. I spent a few hours working on something, and there was a piece of art to show for it, something I could touch and enjoy! What a great feeling it was knowing that here effort equaled results. It's not always like that with writing or with parenting.

I've made lots of stained-glass pieces now. The methodical nature of the process helps me relax and having something tangible to show for my labor lets me tackle the work of writing with greater confidence. And knowing I can access that sense of satisfaction so easily gives me a solid foundation from which I can parent.

moms who take time away from their duties to focus on their own needs are selfish and spoiled, aren't they?

Here's an idea you're probably starting to become familiar with: embrace a little selfishness. You'll be better off for it, and anyway, who cares what anyone else thinks?

From the very second that most women stop doing something productive they start feeling guilty. You're taking a break, but you should be working! What are you doing lazing around? You should always be occupied with something con-

FROM PROBLEM TO SOLUTION

Marie, Mother of Four from Georgia

Marie was tied to her BlackBerry. It would ring, beep, and blink in the middle of a business meeting, a family dinner, a conversation with a close friend, on the soccer field, out for dinner with her husband, while driving kids to activities, or on vacation, and Marie would *always* respond.

One day she found herself typing on her BlackBerry in her tiny bathroom because her kids got so upset when they saw her on it. Sitting on the edge of the tub, she suddenly realized how ridiculous this was. "I decided to really *hear* what the kids were saying," Marie explained. She started leaving the BlackBerry in the car when she got home from work and turning it off when her kids were in the car with her. "It has really helped me and my kids find more peace."

structive. Why? Because that's what we're taught to believe. We snatch a moment here or there, waiting for the big payoff somewhere down the line—when the kids go off to college, when the career quiets down, or when we win the lottery and can stop worrying about money.

But here's the crux: the payoff may never come. There may never be a magical time in the future when your worries are over and you can indulge in those peaceful moments guilt-free, because you won't survive motherhood in one piece. It's a tricky issue: sometimes we don't even realize what we need or want because we're so busy. And we *like* being busy and feeling useful. After all, we're achieving and getting ahead. It makes us feel good—until we lose it.

> A positive attitude may not solve all your problems, but it will annoy enough people to make it worth the effort.
> —Herm Albright, writer

On a morning when juice gets spilled, we shriek at our kids and the intensity of our anger takes us by surprise. A child talks back, and we feel the urge to slap them. (Yup, we know, it's happened to all of us!) Driving to the next play date, we find ourselves suddenly crying. We walk around like automatons, doing all the right things, but unable to feel much emotion except a vague sense of anger and weariness.

The more we do, the more we have to do. There's just no getting on top of it.

The Busywork Won't Stop Until We *Make It Stop*

On a day-to-day basis, even without all the noise that surrounds us—the technology, the cars, the media, the constant buzz of action—we have lots to do as mothers. Sometimes it feels as if our to-do lists don't ever shrink as we check things off, but grow exponentially.

Consider this: we're told from the day we're born that it's sinful to be slothful. We take pride in being a society of doers. But what toll does this take on us? The alarming rise in the rate of sleeping pill usage tells us loud and clear that many of us are finding it harder and harder to relax. According to the National Institutes of Health, up to 40 percent of adult Americans suffer sleep problems each year. Hardly surprising, then, that pharmacists filled forty-three million prescriptions for sleep drugs in 2005—that's up 32 percent in only four years, according to *Consumer Reports*. Without medication, the mind stays in overdrive and can't achieve rest. Yet our bodies *need* rest. (Did you know that sleep deprivation is one of the most effective forms of torture?) At a certain point, even if our minds haven't yet acknowledged it, we break down physically and mentally.

> *It is quite gratifying to feel guilty if you haven't done anything wrong: how noble! Whereas it is rather hard and certainly depressing to admit guilt and repent.*
> —Hannah Arendt, philosopher

Yet we're told over and over again that more is better. All three of us sure fell into *that* trap: We'll be "happier" and more "successful" if we do and have more. A more active social life makes us feel more tapped in. More meetings at work are a sign of how much we're needed. More places to be during the day means we are active, engaged, and living life fully. But it's an illusion. The busier we are, the less we're able to savor the simple aspects of mothering—and of ourselves—that can bring us such joy.

We know that when we are calm and centered, we become better humans. Yet we persist in pushing our needs aside, at great risk to ourselves and our families. The following are only some of the negative consequences of not granting ourselves downtime:

► **Physical depletion.** We suffer headaches, backaches, and stomachaches. At the end of a long day, Katrin often develops splitting headaches. She's learned this is a clear sign for her to look at her schedule and cut her activities in half.

► **Loss of mental capacity.** Leah, a businesswoman from Massachusetts, told us that when she hasn't had a moment of peace, she can't concentrate in her meetings. Even spending only ten minutes a day being alone or in an activity of her choice helps her brain stay sharp.

► **Impatience.** Who hasn't felt that swell of irritation at a benign request, or snapped at a child's guileless mistake? Susan recognized that when she was being snippy with her kids, it was time to give *herself* a break.

► **Strained relationships.** When we're tired, cranky, or argumentative, our interactions with family, friends, coworkers, spouses, teachers and our own beloved children—everyone, in other words—suffers.

► **Poor role-modeling for our kids.** They learn by our example and feel the pace we set. Mothers are the pulse of the household. When Anne started running at a pace that was too hard to keep up, she realized that her kids felt it, too.

Guilt: It's Just a Big, Fat Excuse

Even though almost anyone can recognize the negative effects of running on empty—and the positive effects of feeling appreciated and centered—lots of mothers out there can't seem to make downtime a reality. Why? Almost 100 percent of the women we talked to cited two reasons. The first is that they simply don't believe they have the spare time.

But the second is the real clincher: they feel guilty. According to a 2006 ABC News poll, 52 percent of mothers say they suffer from parental guilt—mostly because they worry that they don't spend enough time with their kids.

We were amazed by how many women accepted guilt as a fact of life for a parent—they would continue suffering through it, unable to get rid of it. Many of us believe we've got to sacrifice ourselves for our children and families or we're failing at our most important calling, so we are quick to feel guilty for the slightest time-out we might give ourselves. Failure to do something well—especially when related to impressionable, vulnerable, needy kids—always results in guilt. But there's a more insidious reason we suffer like this, and it's a tough one to face.

Guilt actually makes us feel better. It's a way to do what we want and justify it to ourselves. If we at least can feel guilty about having done something selfish, it makes the action itself

FROM PROBLEM TO SOLUTION

Linda, Mother of Three from Arizona

One day Linda thought she was losing her mind. She locked herself in her car and turned on the music full blast. After a few minutes she started to feel better. "But then I got antsy," she said. "Even in my total freak-out I started feeling guilty about sitting around doing nothing!" So she tried an experiment: when she felt herself losing her cool, she gave herself a time-out by setting the oven timer. Then she told the kids she'd be in the car for ten minutes and not to bother her unless the house was burning down. Turning up the music, she closed her eyes. She discovered it was a great way to shake herself out of a mood, and now the kids love to tease her about her ever-more-frequent "Mom time-outs!"

less bad. Sure, this seems like a contradiction—who wants to feel guilty, you may ask? But let's be brutally honest: how much guilt do you experience about things that you know are simply not worthy of it? The reason you continue to sneak off and have the occasional lunch with the girls or watch that stupid movie instead of sorting the moving boxes is because you need it. Guilt is one of those emotions that's often more harmful than the action that caused the guilt in the first place. Wasting time and goodwill on allowing guilt to fester about small things is simply destructive. It's really just an excuse not to change your behavior.

The Quandary of the Working Mother

Working moms carry the burden of guilt with them constantly, and it's nothing to be sniffed at. When you can see in your child's eyes the unmet desire to have more time with you, how could you not feel guilty? The question here isn't so much whether guilt is warranted or useful but whether there's anything we can do about it. How can the busy, loving mom who works outside the home find a way to take care of herself when she's already away at work so many hours a day? If she gets time away from home and family anyway, does she really need personal time-outs?

Denise from Washington, D.C., mother of a toddler, shared this with us: "I'm so stressed at work all the time—I have such a relentless, go-go-go kind of job. So when it comes to vacation time, I dream of playing golf, not hanging out with my little guy. But how can I justify that when I'm gone so much?"

Often there's tangible tension between stay-at-home moms and working mothers in this department. Working moms look at those lucky women who get to be with their kids at home with a mixture of jealousy and disdain. *They* don't have to go to work—they get to relax at the playground, do some laundry, have coffee with friends, and help with homework. Their time is their own! Stay-at-home mothers, on the other hand, feel they need to justify their existence because it seems like they're not accomplishing much on a day-to-day basis. To them, working mothers are the fortunate ones, entering the sanctuary of an office full of adults every day, having a reason to dress nicely, and using their brains for something other than finding the missing shoes.

> *Within yourself is a stillness and a sanctuary to which you can retreat at any time and be yourself.*
> —Hermann Hesse, novelist

Of course, the reality is that each approach to life—and thereby parenting—has its merits, and the grass-is-greener mentality doesn't help solve the problem of guilt. We're all just women trying to do a good job as mothers. Whether we're employed or not, whether we believe we have "free" time or not, a priority for us as mothers must be finding a way to step away from the mayhem momentarily.

How Are We Supposed to Pull It Off?

The only way we can persuade you that downtime isn't an option but a necessity is by having you face up to the reasons you're currently not making it happen. We've heard every single one of these reasons in the focus groups we've held. And believe us, we know personally, because during our decade of friendship, we've complained to each other ad nauseam using each and every one of these excuses:

SUSAN'S BURIED UNDER HER OWN PILES

You walk into my kitchen and the first thing you see is my calendar. It takes up half a wall, and it's one of those wipe-'em-clean ones where I can squeeze just about anything in. Usually, it's chockablock with color-coded messages, appointments, and notes. I was used to juggling things at the office, and now that I'm at home I like to know exactly who needs me, when, and where.

A few springs ago, my aunt and I were out walking together. A life coach, she'll always listen patiently to me and then come out with a zinger that puts everything in perspective.

I was limping along—I'd just had knee surgery—talking about my work. I probably talked for twenty minutes straight about working with the kids, working with the teachers, working to get the bedrooms sorted, working on eating more healthfully, and so on.

At the end of my speech, she looked at me. "Susan," she said gently, "what's all this *work* you're talking about?"

I was a little put out. "Well, the work of running the family. You know? It's work. It's hard."

She shook her head. "Why are you working so hard?" she asked. "What would happen if you stopped 'working'?"

I thought about what she meant: Why was I calling everything I did work? Why was I working myself so hard? What was I trying to prove? And to whom? If I changed my outlook—the words I used—would it change my life? I realized that I was running myself off my feet "working"—so much so that my health was beginning to take a beating from trying to please other people.

I decided to try something new that I had read about. I set the alarm a little early the next day to try meditation. Very slowly, I got out of bed; the house was quiet (the kids were still asleep and my husband was long gone). I lay right on the floor and started to focus on my breathing while I was waking up. I took some deep, slow inhales and exhales and really concentrated on the breaths, trying to stay in a relaxed state. As I began to wake up, my mind started to bounce about to all the things I had to do and I had to really concentrate to keep it blank and clear.

After doing the early morning meditation for a few days in a row, I got the hang of it. In fact, at night before falling asleep, I started to really look forward to it. Now my calendar has more blank spots in it and more reminders to myself to take five.

▶ There's just no time for it.

▶ Insisting that we need time for ourselves makes us feel indulgent and selfish. We don't like other people thinking of us as needy.

▶ It's hard not to feel guilty about taking time-outs, and since guilt is so annoying, we'd rather just ignore our needs.

▶ No one understands that we need quiet time. Our spouses think they don't need it, so why should we? Our kids certainly don't think we deserve it. And we're much too tired to justify it.

▶ We want to be all things to all people at all times. Admitting we can't cope unless we pamper ourselves makes us feel like sissies.

▶ We stay at home with the kids, so we feel the need to justify our existence with constant work.

▶ Since we work outside the home, we want to spend as much of our free time with our kids as possible, and we feel like we're cheating them and ourselves if we don't.

▶ When we're still, we have to face our inner demons. This can be really scary. If we keep busy, we never need to face up to what's really going on inside.

▶ It's much too expensive to keep paying for babysitters so that we can lounge around getting in touch with our inner selves.

Heike, a mother of two from Germany, told us that her husband is on the road all week, so taking time for herself on the weekends feels totally unjustifiable as it's more time away from *him*.

Bottom line: every woman can find a million reasonable-sounding excuses not to focus on herself. But in the long run, it sets you up for failure.

> *Then I thought of reading—the nice and subtle happiness of reading . . . this joy not dulled by age, this polite and unpunishable vice, this selfish, serene, lifelong intoxication . . .*
> —Logan Pearsall Smith, writer

No time to relax: that's certainly how we've felt. Here are some of the things we tried that might be helpful for you:

▶ **What works?** Determine a handful of activities that make you feel peaceful. Some might be quick, others time consuming. This is about what works for you. Adele, a mother of two from Boston, discovered she loves puzzles because the methodical nature of putting them together calms her mind down.

▶ **When to do it.** Brainstorm possible pockets of time. You may have to weed things out of your daily to-do list. Could you get up a little earlier, take a lunch break, disappear while the kids are doing homework or while your spouse is clearing dinner, clean up less, drive less, make fewer family commitments, or trade watching kids with a friend or two, so each can have time to herself?

▶ **Get support.** Explain to your partner why this is important to your well-being and how he or she can help you realize your goal. Share the many ways it makes you a better mother and partner. Get your kids to back you up, by giving them concrete examples of how great they feel when they've had a chance to unwind.

▶ **Spread the love.** Make sure everyone reaps the benefits of your newly energized and centered self. Say "Thank you" often; show your gratitude with generosity.

▶ **Schedule it.** Mark your downtime on a communal calendar.

▶ **Analyze your actions.** If you're falling into a pattern of skipping your designated time alone, ask yourself why. Have you chosen an activity that isn't quite right for you? Are you trying to be "good" rather than really doing what you want, which can be absolutely nothing—that counts too!

Sometimes women make the wrong assumptions about why quiet time is impossible. Maybe they don't actually know what would make them feel good. Most often, they believe they don't even have ten minutes to spare, when what they really need is encouragement to think creatively. Kristen from Delaware realized that she could take fifteen minutes at night to soak in the bathtub if she ran the water while she read to her two kids—

with the added hidden benefit of giving her an excuse to call it quits after one or two books.

For some women, the effort they put into finding themselves by taking time-outs from mothering can become an eye-opening process. Over the years, many women grow to define themselves through their children or their work, and when faced with a big, blank spot in their schedule, they may not like what they see: emptiness inside themselves, lack of a sense of purpose, and no interests. We came across a mother of three with a life many people would die for—great big apartment in New York, cute kids, nice cars, plenty of money for renovation, and vacations and nice dinners out—but who feels so lost when her kids are at school that she spends all her time shopping. Carmen, mother of two from Indiana, said, "Boredom is formative. When I'm bored, I'm pushed to look deep inside myself, and it's actually good for me."

Back to Basics

Rediscovering old pastimes can give you lots of ways to take a break from everyday reality and enjoy some downtime. Once upon a time were you enthralled by movies? Join an online DVD rental service such as Netflix, and watch a rental once a week. Did you love going to coffeehouses and writing in a journal? Drop off the kids early, and take half an hour for a latte and the morning paper. When you were younger, did you love tennis? Join up with a friend, and hit a few balls once a week.

For some women, an activity as simple as filing papers, balancing a checkbook, filling out a spreadsheet, or cleaning a drawer can be immensely rewarding and peaceful. The key is to find what works for you.

Explore the different ways to find activities you like, and pay close attention to how they make you feel—you can try writing about it in your *Woman's Workbook*. When one doesn't fit the bill, try another. Start slowly, and build up. When you find what really calms you down, you'll know it.

Just think of the gift this passes on to your children: seeing you consciously step back from workaday stress teaches them ways to handle the strains they'll encounter in their own lives.

FROM PROBLEM TO SOLUTION

Elise, Mother of Two from Washington, D.C.

Elise, a pediatrician, used to be a rocker in the good old days and decided she desperately needed more music in her life. She made some calls to old friends and now has a jam band come over every month to practice in the basement of her townhouse. It's not a fancy setup: they're squeezed in among the boxes, pipes, and dust. But the band members' kids all play together upstairs, and the grownups get to be as loud as they want. "I can feel my muscles loosening up as soon as I pick up that guitar," she said. "It's like I'm a teenager again!"

Every mother wants her kids to discover who they are and live that life to the fullest, to have passions outside school, to understand how to handle life's relentless pace. Learning those skills starts right at home with you—the fulfilled, rested mother.

> *Be more splendid, more extraordinary.*
> *Use every moment to fill yourself up.*
> —Oprah Winfrey, television host

TIPS FROM THE TRENCHES

▶ **Schedule a weekly date with yourself.** Inspirational speaker and writer Julia Cameron advocates committing to "Artist's Dates" for ourselves. This involves determining which peaceful and solitary activity makes us happy—going to a bookstore, biking, looking at a painting— and giving ourselves permission to indulge in this activity *once a week.* Cameron argues that if you make and keep this one- to three-hour date each and every week for two months, you will soon rediscover a sense of vitality and patience.

▶ **Find a peaceful sport.** How often have you been in an exercise class or at the end of a long run and instead of feeling energized, you're frazzled and exhausted? Or are you a couch potato, intimidated by new-age activities because you just don't think you're the right type? Consider investing some time in a physical activity that is peaceful as well as healthy, such as yoga, Pilates, or walking. This can give our minds nourishment and rest, while gently awakening our bodies.

▶ **Cut down on noise levels at home and in the car.**
Just because we're used to having the television on all the time
doesn't mean we can't live without it. Experiment with turning the TV off during the week. You'll probably find that
although they'll initially kick and scream, the children will
end up filling their time with other activities. Sometimes in
the car, the long ads on the commercial radio stations or loud
music, together with the kids' bickering, can whip you into
a real frenzy. Switching off background noise can lead to an
immediate reduction in low-grade stress.

▶ **Read the newspaper every day.** It's breakfast, and the
kids are demanding juice, finishing homework, or crying about
the huge tangle in their hair—you wish you had eight arms.
Try something radical. What would happen if, when the kids
came to the table, you had the juice and cereal out and were
sitting peacefully reading the newspaper? Turn off the TV or
computer, and get your news from a paper. When the kids
demand a spoon or ask where their jackets are, you calmly look
up from your article and say, "Honey, I'm reading the paper."

▶ **Dedicate one room as a quiet zone.** Often our apart-
ments and houses are overwhelmed by the noises and possessions of the little people. It's not unreasonable to carve out a
little space for yourself where you can be quiet. Maybe it's a
comfortable chair you can retreat to in your bathroom, where
no one may enter on pain of death. Or maybe you can designate
a whole room as a no-ruckus zone. Make a sign for the door,
find new homes for half of the belongings crammed in there,

and banish TVs and video games and anything that makes a constant electronic buzz.

▶ **Write out affirmations for yourself.** Some people find the process of writing affirmations hokey. But so much of a mother's job (like that of an artist) involves effort without immediate results, so we need to remind ourselves of our goals and our successes. Try waking up in the morning and instead of tackling a to-do list, write out five affirmations that relate to work, family, or self. An example is, "I am a kind and imaginative mother, who helps her kids think outside the box." When you've found a few you're happy with, repeat them to yourself each morning.

▶ **Reawaken your interest in music.** Many mothers get into a rut with music. They don't have the same taste as their kids or their spouse, it's been decades since they've attended a concert, and they hate all the new stuff out there. But admitting music—*your* music—back into your life can be hugely invigorating. When you're sitting together as a family at breakfast, at dinner, or after school, try turning on classical music instead of the TV or radio. In the car, put in a CD of old favorites and crank the volume. Surf the Internet for music sites, and buy some interesting tunes. Ask your friends what they like to listen to. Open your mind to new sounds.

▶ **Use visualization to determine your needs.** We may know it's important to do something, yet still not do it. In the heat of the moment, we push it aside. When you catch yourself doing this, close your eyes. Imagine you're doing the activity you so cavalierly dismissed. How will you feel if you do it? Will it add something good to your day? This can help determine your priorities. Equally, if you're freaking out at the kids and you can't seem to shake your anger, imagine a chair in the middle of a quiet, empty room. You may need to leave the children for a moment and mentally place yourself on that chair until you're in better control.

▶ **Get the most from an evening out.** You've organized a night out with friends, your partner, or alone. The babysitter is coming at 7 P.M. You've sprung for the sitter, why not make it really worthwhile by getting the sitter to come an hour early? You can indulge in a nice, long prep time (e.g., shaving your legs, applying makeup, doing your hair, picking the right outfit) so you go out feeling on top of the world, or you could even fit in a tryst with your husband before you both get too exhausted! You'd be amazed at how preemptive lovemaking can turn a normal evening out into a wonderful opportunity for togetherness.

▶ **Look for inspiration in ordinary places.** Sometimes we overlook the simple things in life because we expect that finding pleasure will be more complicated than it really is. Sitting on a train, pruning trees, watching clouds shift, reading junky magazines, organizing our books, lying on a bed and falling into a doze, listening to the crickets—these basic, easy-to-do activities can bring genuine joy. Whether you consistently take a few minutes to savor these small pleasures or spend an entire day reveling in them, they'll fill you up with renewed energy without you having to invest a huge amount of effort or money.

I TRIED THE TIPS! PAULINE, MOTHER OF TWO FROM VERMONT

"The newspaper idea totally worked for me. I've been at least picking up the newspaper every morning at breakfast. Sometimes I only get through the first page, but other mornings I find myself into the Living and Arts section. It's baby steps, but the kids seem to expect it now. Believe it or not, I think me being settled in one place sets a calmer tone in the household. Every now and then, we'll even have a conversation about something I'm reading. Then I think, yeah, I'm taking time for myself *and* teaching them something!"

THE LOVING LINK WITH YOUR PARTNER

From Living Side by Side to
Integrating Your Life Together

Are you one of those well-meaning mothers who overservices her children, always assessing, planning, organizing, worrying? Do you focus so much attention on your kids and your home that you sometimes forget about that guy over there in the corner? You know the one we mean—your husband.

There's another very real casualty of hovering mothering (aside from the mom herself and the children) and that's the husband. We're all focusing so much attention on our kids, making up for the time we're at work or frantically trying to be the best, most diligent mothers we can be, that it's easy to slip into the mode of practically ignoring the men in our lives. Or we only pay attention to them when they irritate us, which seems to happen all too often.

When you have too much on your plate already, it's hardly surprising that finding time to really connect with the other half of the parental equation seems almost impossible. In your heart, you know it's important, but reality gets in the way. You're stressed, you're tired, you're annoyed with his seeming lack of empathy—you forget the beauty of the love you shared when life was less complicated. Penny from North Carolina, mother of three, said she often stares at her husband as he plays with the kids, trying to think back to when they first fell in love. "It's good to make the connection between who he is today with who he was before," she said, "so I can recognize the good things, not just bitch about the bad."

> *The way to love anything is to realize that it might be lost.*
> —G. K. Chesterton, writer

Parenting with a like-minded partner who shares the joys and the challenges of life as an adult is an unbelievable gift. If you've got someone in your corner, someone who really wants what's best for you, it's a lot easier to be a fulfilled, rather than perennially frustrated, woman and mother. Ultimately, a good relationship with your coparent is the key to being able to successfully stay in touch with your own needs while also fulfilling the needs of your family.

Those of us in committed relationships can consider ourselves lucky! Every woman starting a family dreams of having a sympathetic ear and a helping hand at the ready, someone who knows her better than she knows herself, not to mention lights her fire, romantically speaking. Yet this sometimes seems an all-too-elusive dream. According to the U.S. Census Bureau, families run by single mothers rose from 3.4 million in 1970 to more than 10 million in 2003—a trend that's evident across Europe and Australia as well. Why this sharp increase? It's because of a lethal combination of high expectations, neglect, and lack of communication, a modus operandi you can slip into without even noticing it.

> *All weddings are similar, but every marriage is different.*
> —John Berger, writer

Humans are better, happier beasts when their personal, emotional needs are being met. "Cerebral virtues—curiosity, love of learning—are less strongly tied to happiness than interpersonal virtues like kindness, gratitude, and capacity for love," says Dr. Martin Seligman, author of *Authentic Happiness*. It's the gentleness and appreciation that couples share in their best moments that nourishes them in a way nothing else can. Most mothers in our outreach felt their husbands were just as frantic as they were, trying to figure out their new position in life's hierarchy; cramming work, family, and love into an overly busy schedule; and often feeling maligned or ignored by their tired-out wives. Noel from California, mother of three, said it best: "*We* want to be perfect, and we want *them* to be perfect. When these guys just can't do it, we imagine they're being willfully annoying!" Time and again, women said their husbands complain to them about being treated like children who can never do anything to quite the right standard.

Here we speak to the woman trying to raise children with a partner—whether it's a he or a she, a husband or long-term romantic cohort—and finds that instead of sharing intimacy and delight, she's simply splitting the burdens of day-to-day living with another warm body. From talking to mothers with toddlers to those with teenagers, and everything in between, it was quickly obvious to us that most modern couples engage in this frustrating struggle to find a balanced approach to parenting. We're all trying to find our feet.

Finding Your Groove

How couples operate can be pretty mysterious. What works for one is disastrous for another. Ever been away on a trip with another couple and wondered how on earth they manage? Observing someone else's rhythms, watching the give-and-take (or just the give!) and wondering how they can stand each other's foibles can be very illuminating. Some have financial struggles but have never been happier; some have all the money in the world but can't stop fighting. Sometimes you might envy their relationship; sometimes you wonder how they make it through the day without screaming, "Get me out of here!"

Of course, there's no blueprint for how to be happy in your marriage. Whether you met and fell in love as youngsters, ex-

FROM PROBLEM TO SOLUTION

Evie, Mother of Two from Massachusetts

Evie quit her job to stay home with her kids. Her husband, Sam, travels a lot for work, and whenever he's home, he just wants to chill out eating hot dogs and watching TV. Meanwhile she's chomping at the bit; it drives Evie nuts. "Our needs are so different, I get frustrated," she said. "It's sometimes hard to imagine them ever lining up again." Then Sam was laid off for a few months and spent that time at home with her, being part of the ebb and flow of Evie's everyday life. "He saw *why* I needed what I needed, and he started trying to give it to me in bits and pieces. That helped me lay off him, too. Now we seem to understand where we're coming from again."

pecting life to be one long fairy tale, or connected as more-established adults, with children or stepchildren in tow, your relationship with your mate will change over time. Not might, *will.* If there isn't any room for growth and change, you'll be in for some serious heartache.

In many ways, watching your husband become a father is the most beautiful sight in the world. You'll learn things about him that you never knew before. When you look at your children, you'll see his qualities reflected in them. It's an amazing progression.

But truthfully, it can be a hard one too. Suddenly he comes last on your list of priorities, somewhere before taking out the trash but after unloading the dishwasher—and certainly way after your work responsibilities.

As many of you probably know from experience, the number one thing couples fight about is finances—and then sex (more on *that* later). Life as an adult is full of financial, emotional, and physical responsibilities, so it's no surprise we fight about money. The old days when Mom sat at the kitchen table with no idea how much money was in the bank are long gone. Nowadays it's not really about sharing evenly in all this management; it's about being aware and taking ownership of the issues. What's important is to try to operate as a team in which each partner agrees on a process for handling incoming and outgoing funds, spending and saving each month, and managing major investments, debts, or acquisitions.

How important is it to *you* to have some—or total—financial independence? That's for each couple to decide. But facing up to reality is a must, and doing it as a team will make it much more palatable.

Dreams and Reality

If you've ever watched a soap opera, read a romance novel, or seen a chick flick, you most likely have unrealistic expectations about marriage and relationships. According to these sources, they're supposed to be full of thrills, romance, wealth, and of course, lots of heart-pounding sex. But countless marriages become fractured or end in divorce because of these unrealistic expectations. In 2004, the National Marriage Project at Rutgers University conducted a report whose key finding was, "For the average couple marrying in recent years, the lifetime probability of divorce or separation remains close to 50 percent."

Here's the good news: many mothers gave us tons of insight into how to achieve better teamwork and greater intimacy. From the information we gathered, the main cornerstones of a realistic modern relationship boil down to:

► **Partnership.** You're a team, and members of a team back each other up, help each other out, and have each other's best interests at heart.

► **Communication and compromise.** It's sometimes a pain to have to spell things out, but it's important to state your case and make sure you know his, and then be willing to meet somewhere in the middle.

► **Trust and respect.** Without trust it's hard to open up and allow yourself to be vulnerable. When there's mutual respect, any challenge can be more easily overcome.

► **Intimacy.** Being physically connected encourages tenderness, sincerity, and empathy.

► **Having fun together.** Life is short, and having fun is good!

How often do we get sidetracked by our many responsibilities and forget to have fun with our mates? We disregard the joy of being intimate. We overlook the simple happiness of silently walking together, hand in hand. Is it really so hard to rediscover the bonds you shared with your husband when you were both still wide-eyed and full of hope? Some ideas we uncovered in our outreach for ways to reconnect are:

▶ **Sleep in a strange bed.** With him! If there's any way you can pull it off, the number one way to reconnect is by spending time together away from the hubbub of ordinary life. Try going to a hotel or borrowing a friend's country cottage for a night.

▶ **Do it as a couple.** Join a salsa class, take cooking lessons, or find a shared creative outlet that gets you out of the house together.

▶ **Spice up your date nights.** Instead of dinner and a movie, go to a cabaret, a concert, a book reading, or a horse race.

▶ **Get sweaty together.** Go running or try hot yoga. Ella, mother of two from California, started sailing regularly once every weekend with her husband (an activity they'd *loved* when they started dating).

▶ **Sneak out.** A short walk late at night after the kids are in bed or early in the morning before they get up, can be totally invigorating. What's key is time alone together.

> What counts in making a happy marriage is not so much how compatible you are, but how you deal with incompatibility.
> —Leo Tolstoy, writer

Say What You Mean and Mean What You Say

No doubt about it, women want men to be more intuitive. When you're tired after work and are calming a frantic child, you want your husband—of his own accord—to set the table, clear the cleats from underfoot, or simply ask, "Is there anything I can do?"

Wouldn't it be great if men were mind readers? The reality is that this may be too much to ask. If we want something from our partners, we better get used to asking for it. Terrence Real, author of *How Can I Get Through to You*, puts it this way: "We give lip service to the idea that marriage takes effort, but in our day-to-day lives we think, I don't want to work this hard."

I think men who have a pierced ear are better prepared for marriage. They've experienced pain and bought jewelry.
—Rita Rudner, comedian

So if your guy is obtuse, what can you do about it? Instead of assuming anything, just spell it out. Donna from Vermont told us about sitting at dinner every night with her husband, Gary, and their three kids and always looking longingly at the fridge, hoping Gary would get the hint that it was his job to pour drinks for everyone. Finally, she broke down and yelled at him to get up and do his share. "He couldn't have been more surprised," she said, laughing. "He had no idea what I'd been thinking!" Taking out the guesswork will make things clearer for everyone, and your husband won't have to wonder why

FROM PROBLEM TO SOLUTION

Kristina, Stepmother of One and Mother of Three from California

Kristina came to her second marriage with all sorts of expectations based on her previous experiences. With her ex-husband, she'd often work herself to the bone thinking she was making him happy, only to feel resentful that he didn't appreciate her efforts. Her new husband had a totally different personality, and they had to learn a whole new vocabulary to communicate their needs clearly. "I really worked at it, because I'd already been through one major failure," she explained. "So I left nothing to chance: I made sure we were super clear with each other and didn't take anything for granted."

you've got that funny look on your face, and how he managed to disappoint you once again.

Let's Talk About Sex!

Oh boy, in our focus groups, we could have talked for months on end about the effect that children have on romance. "Children seem to be a growing impediment for the happiness of marriages," according to the Rutger's marriage study. From nursing, wakeful babies to sulking, time-consuming teenagers, moms and dads certainly have less time and patience for romance. These issues can often be short-term, but sometimes they linger long after the kids have learned to tie their own laces. According to a 2004 ABC "Primetime Live" poll, only one-third of couples who've been together more than ten years say their sex life is very exciting, and the percentage of couples having sex two to three times a week plummets from 72 percent in their early years together to only 32 percent after a decade.

Many mothers admitted to feeling guilty that they experienced a slowdown—and let's face it, sometimes a *dead stop*—in their sex drives after having children. As many of us have experienced, the warmth of a tiny baby's body and the nurturing, cuddling, affection they require and return often fill our needs enough that we no longer seek that kind of intimacy from our husbands.

> *The true feeling of sex is that of a deep intimacy,*
> *but above all of a deep complicity.*
> —James Dickey, poet

Sometimes women come to believe that because they don't feel a whole lot of desire, they don't need sex anymore. Since they no longer see themselves as sexual beings, it doesn't take long for sex to become a chore they resist. Well, here's a sobering thought: "Unsatisfying sexual relationships are the all-too-frequent causes of alienation, infidelity, and divorce," according to sex therapist Michelle Weiner-Davis. In her book *The Sex-Starved Marriage*, she says, "Just do it. Desire is a decision.

Once the low-interest partner allows him/herself to be touched and aroused, this will trigger a strong desire to continue being sexual."

Sex with your partner isn't just about satisfying his needs; while that's sometimes the case, it won't always be. It's about rediscovering what you want and need so that you can be whole again. If you're at a stalemate with your man about how often you should be having sex, consider this:

- ► How much intimacy do *you* need in order to feel connected to your husband? Be honest with yourself, because it may be more than you realize. Think back to how you've felt about your spouse during dry periods, and how great you feel when you're being intimate frequently.
- ► How much sex does *he* need to feel content and connected? For most men, intimacy is inexorably connected with sex.
- ► Is there a way you can compromise on frequency, maybe by changing your routines or spicing things up? According to the "Primetime Live" poll, people who call themselves sexually adventurous are more apt—by nearly thirty percentage points—to call their sex lives very exciting and are "considerably more likely in turn to be satisfied with their overall relationship."
- ► The more you do it, the more you'll desire it. Honestly, it's that simple!

FROM PROBLEM TO SOLUTION

Lindsay, Mother of Three from England

When Lindsay and Ian are home together in the evenings, he lies on the couch to unwind while she prepares food and does the bedtime routine. "I do dinner, clean up, and haul myself to bed at 10éÈ È," Lindsay said, "and *then* he's ready for sex. Meanwhile, I'm about as far from the right mood as a person could be!" Realizing that she was resisting Ian more because of how irritating it was that he wasn't plugging into the family than because of a lack of interest in sex, she now makes sure they go out together a few times a month and really connect. "We still need to work on the old nighttime dynamic, but at least we squeeze some good times in there, too."

Some couples need sex every other night, some once a week, some twice a month. Marsha, mother of one from New York, said her boyfriend often goes for months without making a move, and they constantly fight about his disinterest, while Jeannie, a mother of two from New Mexico, told us her husband insists that sex three times a week is the norm. The bottom line is, what each couple needs to feel deeply connected varies so widely that there is simply no norm.

But one thing's for sure: sex matters. One of the primary conclusions drawn from an international survey conducted by the University of Chicago in 2006 was that "subjective sexual well-being was correlated with overall happiness in both men and women." And get this: according to a 2004 study in the National Bureau of Economic Research working papers, increasing frequency of sex from once a month to once a week improves happiness as much as getting a raise of $50,000 a year!

Sex is emotion in motion.
—Mae West, actress

Making love can undoubtedly be great fun, but did you also realize how good it is for your health? A 2004 *Time* magazine article points out that frequent sexual activity can:

► Improve the health of your heart by increasing aerobic fitness (having sex burns the same number of calories as a fifteen- to thirty-minute run)
► Help you ward off pain through the release of endorphins and corticosteroids
► Improve your ability to heal through stimulating an increase in the levels of certain antibodies and oxytocin
► Protect against breast and prostate cancers
► Lower depression rates, thanks to the release of huge amounts of oxytocin before orgasm

So keep those major advantages in mind as you read the top four lame excuses that we've heard or (dare we admit) that we've used once too often ourselves:

1. **"The kids are always around."** How about organizing play dates for them on a weekend afternoon?
2. **"I'm way too tired."** Forget sex at night, and try mornings instead; or sneak off for a quickie (after locking your bedroom door) while the kids are otherwise occupied.
3. **"I just don't have time."** Come on, you can make time for anything if you really want to!
4. **"I don't enjoy it anymore."** Work on figuring out what will spark your lust—maybe it's watching a cute actor in a movie, trying out a sex toy, wearing something pretty to bed, or having more alone-time with your husband *without* sex being involved.

In a June 2003 *Newsweek* article, writer Erica Jong says, "In our post-sexual revolution era, we expect carnality and familiarity wrapped in the same shiny gift package." These expectations are often dashed once real life intervenes, but luckily that doesn't have to spell disaster. "Sex is not the only thing that keeps people together," Jong adds. "Talking and laughing keep couples together. Shared goals keep couples together."

To Each His Own

It's no fun just living side by side with your man. Of course, there will be times when you're in sync and other times when you'll wonder what you ever saw in him. Anna, mother of four

KATRIN LEARNS LIFE IS LONG

During labor, my son Peter was jammed behind my pelvis, unable to slip out—like a polite, accommodating firstborn should—and no amount of pushing would get that behemoth out. Finally, with a big rip, he arrived. The nurses gasped: he was huge—almost ten pounds!

Remember reading in your pregnancy books how *above all else* you don't want a fourth-degree tear from your vagina to your rectum? Remember how you thought, oh no, not me, I will rub vitamin E oil on there, I will get a tiny incision if I absolutely must. Well, that's just what I thought till Peter emerged.

After I'd recovered a bit, my doctor informed me I'd needed loads of stitches. Not one or two, but loads. Then she dropped the bomb. "It's going to take a long time to heal," she said. "It's a bit like a Caesarean section; you might find it takes six months before you can have sex again without pain."

Pain—six months—no sex! She may not have used those exact words. Maybe she was more gentle—I don't remember for sure, I was much too busy wailing.

I looked over at Kevin and felt total despair. I was afraid of the changes a baby would bring into our lives. It had already been months since we'd been intimate. I felt like I wasn't a human being anymore: I *craved* my old body, and I wanted to know that I'd be having hot, passionate sex again one day in the not-too-distant future. I even felt kind of guilty: maybe if I hadn't become such a house, Peter would have come out smaller and I wouldn't have torn so badly.

Kevin just smiled at me. "It's a long life, sweetie," he said.

"But . . . but . . . six months!"

"That's nothing. It'll come and go. One day we'll be old together."

I've thought back to that day a lot in the past fourteen years. We've had our dry spells, our hot and heavy spells, and our regular, ho-hum spells, but all throughout, I have known it's all just a phase. When I start to overanalyze, I try to always remember that image of the two of us, old and wrinkled, still having sex or maybe not. But it's a long, long life. No point being impatient.

from Illinois, tries to make a point of noticing and commenting on the helpful things her husband does, not just telling him when he hasn't cleaned the counters properly or put his shoes away in the right place. She told us she *likes* who she is when she's with him. He brings out qualities in her that make her feel good. When women remind themselves often of the sweet things their husband does and appreciate his efforts, it takes the sting out of disappointments.

Remember that love is not leisure, it is work.
—Anna Quindlen, writer

Mothers understand firsthand the positive benefits of being shown some appreciation. We seek this kind of validation for the invisible work we do all the time. Sometimes it's

FROM PROBLEM TO SOLUTION

Pat, Mother of Three from Virginia

Pat spends every free moment driving her kids all over the universe. She was yearning—no, *dying*—for some time alone, but it just wasn't happening. She enlisted the help of her husband, Tom, and they started brainstorming. He suggested he could do the grocery shopping on the weekends and at least take that off her list, but she really needed to get out of the house more. So Tom had this idea: maybe she could shop late at night, listening to her iPod while he put the younger kids to bed and helped the older one finish up his homework. Pat tried it and loved it. "I'm in my own little world, the market is empty, and no one wants anything from me," she said, "and I'd never have thought of it without Tom."

not that we want our husbands to contribute exactly half of the work in the house or with the kids, but that we want and demand to be understood and respected. You get grumpy pretty quickly when you feel like you're being taken for granted—and that goes for husbands, too!

When there's mutual respect in any relationship, misunderstandings and resentments are bound to be less frequent. You and he should both be passionate about your interests because they're what make you come alive. If your husband loves to fish, so be it; *you* may choose to spend time at the yoga studio. If he needs guy time at the pub, you may need girl time at the movies. When you give each other well-deserved time-outs, you can come together as well-rounded and fulfilled individuals, who aren't seeking constant validation from each other.

> *It is not a lack of love, but a lack of friendship that makes unhappy marriages.*
> —Friedrich Nietzsche, philosopher

Nix the Nagging, Push the Positive

We just can't get around this one: we need to nix the nagging! No woman on earth likes to hear herself nag, yet most of us do it all too often. Those men—they just don't help enough, can't do anything right, lack romance and planning skills, and don't measure up. We kvetch and pray they'll be miraculously transformed.

SUSAN'S GIVE-AND-TAKE

Soon after our second child, Cole, was born, I was invited to go away on a girl's weekend. I worried over asking Topher about it, feeling guilty and selfish, but truth be told, I was barely holding it together. I really needed a break.

So in passing, I mentioned it and waited, holding my breath.

Topher immediately agreed that I needed to get away. "I'd love nothing more than for you to get some time with your friends," he said.

Wow, that's all I needed to hear and I already felt better! He was going to take on all of my seemingly insurmountable tasks, and I'd whisk myself away with my friends to sleep, eat, power through loads of magazines, and drink great coffee all day? Deal!

He also made it a point to say, "Don't worry about us one bit, OK? I've got the home front completely covered." That was the greatest gift he could have given me.

Once a year, Topher goes away with his brothers and brother-in-law. He gets his boy yuks out, laughs until he drops, discusses the future and the past, all with his very best friends. I love it when he goes on that trip—he comes back so happy and refreshed, it has an immediate impact on our relationship.

On his last trip away, our kids were fighting like crazy. I was yelling way too much, and worst of all, I was getting no sleep. But when he called to check in, I tried the Topher approach: "Honey," I said, "I've got it. Don't worry about a thing. We're all set—everyone misses you and we can't wait to see you. But don't rush home, you can use the break."

Across thousands of miles, I could imagine Topher's shoulders dropping a little, and I heard the relief in his voice. That was my gift to him.

Topher and I tune into each other on a daily basis, calling or e-mailing constantly—either checking in or making sure the other is aware of something important coming up. Don't get me wrong, there are days we meet up at 6éÈ È and haven't connected once, but then we take the time to eat together and share our stories. From this foundation, we've gained a real respect for one another and a reciprocal relationship has blossomed. I talk, he listens; he talks, I listen; he encourages, I encourage; and so on. Over the years, we've become like a well-practiced piano duet.

Are we really being fair? Most fathers are much more involved than their own fathers were. Sure, they should help, be intuitive and proactive, not take us for granted, and plug into the family emotionally, but when they fail to be perfect, are they doing so on purpose? In our experience, fathers generally want to do the best they can. Suzanna from California arrived at one of our focus groups fuming about how she had tried to help her husband, Joe, deal with the three kids before leaving: showering, feeding, and getting them in their jammies. But Joe was mad at her for being too controlling and barking orders at him, when she thought she was making things easier for him.

> *Love is an expression and assertion of self-esteem, a response to one's own values in the person of another.*
> —Ayn Rand, writer

In our discussions on this topic—which could easily have gone on from dusk to dawn—we identified the following six things to keep in mind when talking with your husband:

- ► Try hard to use accurate language that isn't freighted with other meanings.
- ► Check in with yourself to make sure you're arguing about the real problem, and that you're not actually mad about something else.
- ► Give him a chance: express your expectations out loud before he dashes them.
- ► Listen when he talks, and talk to him in a way that makes him want to listen. (Of course, you should expect him to return the favor!)

- ► Try avoiding phrases like "you never" and "you always." They're bound to make him defensive—and anyway, *is it really true?*
- ► When you're wrong, you've got to admit it—yes, we know, that's almost impossible for most women! If you can't do it in the heat of the moment, tell him you need some time to cool off, and then go back and fess up.

But What About the Kids, the House, the Chores?

Here's the hard and cold truth: mothers do almost twice as much housework as fathers. According to a 2004 Brown University study (in which the vast majority of women were employed full-time and the rest part-time), wives completed thirty-two hours of housework a week compared to their husband's seventeen.

So what gives? Do women care more? Are men lazy? Do mothers assume most of the cleaning, cooking, and child-rearing responsibilities, even when they're employed outside the house, because they're genetically programmed to do so?

Sigh. All we know is, it's exhausting. The work itself is exhausting, and fighting about it is exhausting. (By the way, here's one quick fix: in professor of psychology John Gottman's so-called Love Lab at the University of Washington, he discovered that husbands who take on more household tasks have sex with their wives more frequently. Give your man that information, and see if *that* changes his habits!)

ANNE'S MORNING MAYHEM

When I went back to work, Bruce took over morning duty two days a week. But was I ever slow in letting go of the reins! I just didn't quite believe he could possibly manage everything the way I did. I mean, mornings in every household are busy, but I think ours take the cake. Backpacks, snacks, juice boxes, lunches, notes to school, projects, finding sneakers or the "right" shoes, finishing homework, making breakfast, helping kids find the clothes they want to wear, doing hair, catching the bus. I was about 110 percent sure he'd be forgetting things all the time.

So to be especially helpful, I'd sneak around late at night for a good hour, laying out the outfits that I knew the kids would want to wear, getting the backpacks ready, and leaving an exhaustive written summary of the day ahead. I'd even wake the kids early the next day to brush their hair and help them get dressed. Then I'd sweep through their rooms making beds and picking up a few odds and ends before leaving.

Eventually, my organization started to slip: maybe I was out the evening before or I'd fall asleep with the kids and simply not get to it. Those mornings were crazy. I'd run around the house, barking orders at everyone. Inevitably I wouldn't be able to handle everything, and I'd race out late, yelling reminders at Bruce over my shoulder: "Don't forget Carly's pick-up note. Remember, Jay doesn't like sandwiches for lunch, and remind Meg that she needs her lacrosse stick!"

Often when I got to work, Bruce would call to report on how the morning went. There'd always be one unpredictable twist or another, and he always handled it beautifully. I had to give him credit—he didn't really need my "interference." At the end the day, Jay might be wearing pants that were two sizes too small or Meg's library book would still be sitting on the counter. But Bruce would always say, "Did we all have a good day or not?"

Bruce's way isn't always going to be my way, and my way is not his, and that's OK. When I'm not micromanaging him, he does just fine. In fact, better than fine: some days, I'll come home from work and he'll have been to the market to get more juice boxes, because he noticed we were out—without my having to say a thing!

But this isn't really just about who does what in the house. It's also about our differing approaches to child rearing. It takes time to develop your own parenting style— you yourself know this from experience. Since your children went from nursing, to walking, to talking, to attending school (to talking back!), your own approach has probably evolved *a lot*. During that time, you may have discovered that your parenting style and your husband's diverge much more than you ever thought they would. This can cause day-to-day friction that gets in the way of your relationship; instead of feeling like a team, you're combatants in a never-ending war!

Women we spoke with clued us in about how to avoid at least *some* of these kinds of battles:

- ▶ Your partner has his own style, and though it may not mesh perfectly with yours, it is nonetheless legitimate.
- ▶ If you can come to respect his way, he'll respect yours more.
- ▶ Talk about your shared values and how your joint-parenting approach can reflect those important values.
- ▶ Appreciate how his style may compliment yours, and it will show your kids that there isn't only one way to do things.
- ▶ Agree to disagree if you must, but on important issues, present a united front whether or not you agree fully. Sending mixed messages to children about vital things like drugs, sex, friends, and family rules is confusing (and will cause *you* major headaches).
- ▶ Figure out how your personalities fit with the needs of the household. Georgia from Idaho, mother of two,

splits the family chores with her husband according to who does what best. She deals with daily homework because she has the patience, and her husband handles helping with the longer-term projects because he's more creative.

Almost universally, women admitted to us that they like to call the shots regarding management of the household. It's

FROM PROBLEM TO SOLUTION

Lizzie, Mother of Two from Illinois

Lizzie grew up with strict parents and as a result likes to run a relaxed household. When she's in charge, there's no yelling, not much discipline, and certainly no chore charts or punishments. On the other hand, her husband, Lawrence, is a stickler for details. He likes things tidy and kids well-behaved; he rigorously enforces consequences for bad behavior. "We used to really compliment each other, before kids," Lizzie said. "Then what we'd enjoyed so much about each other became a liability." They had to find a middle ground. With the help of a therapist, they listed their greatest wishes and worst fears regarding parenting and rediscovered their shared values. "We argue a lot less because we know that deep down we do care about the same things."

their way or the highway, and they're often willing to fight to the death about it.

But let's hold on a minute here—is that really the best approach? You could be doing yourself a real disservice by trying so hard to change his ways, because you're probably fighting a losing battle. Try focusing on two or three areas that are most important to you and achieving compromise in all other smaller matters. It's just going to make your life easier to cut him, and yourself, a break.

Loving Your Partner Through Ups and Downs

Of course you want to be happy in your marriage; it will make you a more contented woman and a much better mother. The best way to avoid just co-parenting—perpetually exhausted and out of sync—is to recognize that every relationship has its phases, and to be gentle and forgiving with each other. Marriage therapist Terrence Real explains in his books that committed couples must endure phases of harmony, disharmony, and restoration in order to stay happy together. He argues that as long as we have patience for this continuous cycle, we'll be OK in the long run.

Love is not static, it's ever-evolving. We should try to share old passions, revisit the early days of our love, be generous in our thoughts, share the laughter as well as the hardships, always give praise when praise is due, and make love often and tenderly. There's no quick fix to keeping a relationship healthy, but consistent effort over time with your mate, along with a good dose of reality-checking, can help create a happier home life for everyone.

TIPS FROM THE TRENCHES

▶ **Have a blast together.** This is definitely the number one suggestion that came up. When we get busy, we forget how to have a plain old rockin' good time together. Go on a roller-coaster ride, *together*—not with your children. Hop on bikes. Pack a picnic. Go to a park, and have a sprinting competition. Wash your car together, and get soaking wet. Do something foolish and fun, and remind yourselves that you're not too old to laugh till you wet your pants.

▶ **Break the ice.** It's always awkward to start fooling around when you've been knee deep in dishes, dirty clothes, or bill paying. It doesn't take much to get men going, but for women it's a whole different story. Try using massage oil and getting him to give you a good back rub. Or how about getting all clean and steamy together in the bathroom? Lighting some candles can help reset the mood. Now, guess what we heard is a favorite icebreaker is? Yup, you guessed it, soft porn. Go for it!

▶ **Work on your feminine wiles.** Won't being intimate be a lot more fun if you embrace an open-minded attitude? Maybe trying something new would give you a kick. Think about something you've always wondered about—maybe it's a sex aid, or a risqué movie, or a new technique you've heard about—and do some research. These kinds of forays are easy and private now that we have the Internet.

▶ **Small gestures matter.** Let's not forget how nice it is to be the recipient of small gestures of affection. A quick kiss on the cheek, a rub of your forearm, a pat on the back, a foot massage—all with no strings attached—can really boost your mood. Every time you get the chance, reach out to him with a sweet gesture of love, and you'll soon find him looking at you with renewed appreciation.

▶ **Take time away from each other.** Too much togetherness is not always such a good thing. Sometimes we need time-outs from each other to remember what we love. Maybe you need one morning each weekend to go to a museum, do Pilates, or take a knitting class. Maybe you need a whole night away, visiting an old friend, or a weekend taking a refresher business course with a bunch of strangers. Being an independent woman will make you appreciate all the more the strengths you share when you are together.

▶ **Pick up on cues.** If you're sensitive to his mood and sympathize, he'll return the favor. If he looks tired, suggest he go for a run or take a quick nap. If he's buzzing around stressed out, ask some questions and try to tune into what is *really* going on with him. When it's your turn to be tired or stressed, maybe he'll have learned to take notice.

▶ **Take time to observe.** Instead of focusing on where things are going wrong, observe him at unguarded moments and think about all the things that are right. Do you like the way he smiles when he's doing a puzzle with your eleven-year-old? Is it amusing to see him riding a scooter with your teenager? When he's hauling leaves in the yard or hammering the pipes under the sink, do his muscles remind you of the good old days?

▶ **Take a time-out before launching in.** When it's on the tip of your tongue to lash out, hold back. Force yourself to take a time-out. After five minutes, reassess what you were going to say. Is it still important? If you bring it up later, at a moment when things have calmed down, could your comments be more effective? Is it possible to rephrase your criticism and turn it into a suggestion instead?

▶ **Be curious about him.** Truthfully, it's easy to get tired of our partner's constant talk about work, golf, politics, or whatever rocks his boat at any given time. But try this: instead of just listening (and being mentally absent), *ask him questions.* Each time he answers, ask another one. You'll find that soon you'll be more present in your conversations, and because of that, you'll be more genuinely interested. At the end of the day, you also benefit from feeling more connected.

▶ **Get back to your roots.** When you were first dating, what did you love doing together? Did you go on late-night runs or work out at the gym? Did you catch the Saturday matinees? Would you spend every other weekend hiking in the hills or swimming in the ocean? Were art galleries your favorite place to flirt, or maybe you liked dirt biking or taking walks along the promenade? Reconnect with those activities that brought you together, and enjoy them all over again.

I TRIED THE TIPS! ELIZABETH, MOTHER OF THREE FROM WISCONSIN

"I just got back from a night away with my husband, John, and it was incredible. At first I was nervous we wouldn't connect the way we used to, but the minute we got in the car, we were laughing and gabbing just like old times. It was amazing to be in the moment with John—not rushed, just taking our time. We're going to try to get away once every few months—it's just so good for our marriage. We even have a code word we use when life gets crazy. When we say it, we tap right into that connected feeling we had when we were away!"

THE NEED TO REACH OUT

From Motherhood in Isolation to Creating and Providing a Support Network

It's no secret that women lean heavily on their friends, especially their girlfriends, in order to stay sane. When we just can't take it anymore—the kids are driving us nuts, our husband doesn't get it, our boss is being difficult—it's our friends we turn to. In a 2004 *Time* poll, 63 percent of women said they talk to friends or family to improve their mood. Women want and need to be heard. Go online and search for mothers' groups: if you type in "blogs about mothers," you'll get fifteen million sites.

> *Friendship marks a life even more deeply than love.*
> —Elie Wiesel, Holocaust survivor

When they're stressed, women release the hormone oxytocin, according to Dr. Laura Cousin Klein, assistant professor of biobehavioral health at Penn State University. This hormone encourages them to "tend and befriend" rather than react as men do by fight-or-flight. It's simply written in women's genetic codes to turn toward family and friends when they're under pressure. Finding community makes us feel more powerful. Connecting with friends resets our inner equilibrium.

> If you find out next week that you are terminally ill—and we're all terminally ill on this bus—all that will matter is memories of beauty, that people loved you, and you loved them, and that you tried to help the poor and innocent.
> —Anne Lamott, writer

How many times have you spent a chaotic weekend with your family when your home is a disaster zone, kids are fighting, and chores need to get done but are being ignored by everyone? It's about all you can do to gather up your brood and head over to a friend's for dinner. You've barely said a word to your spouse all day, and your nerves are frayed.

But as soon as you walk through the door of your friend's place, she gives you a hug and a glass of wine, the kids run off to play, you sit down, and aah, you start to relax. Before you know it, you're laughing at yourself and your friend is sharing her own war stories. Suddenly your husband looks human to you again, and you're back to being comfortable in your own skin. Once again, you ask yourself: where would I be without my friends?

For many of us, our husbands or partners provide incredible support that we feel we couldn't live without. But many mothers are divorced or single, and even those in steady relationships find they don't get the same sense of relief and camaraderie gabbing with their mates as they do with their girlfriends. It's just different!

Your own extended family is usually a natural ally, and for some it's the first place they turn. But often family members live far away, or carry complex emotional baggage that makes it hard to rely on them as you might rely on friends. If family members are at different stages of their lives, they may not always be able to relate to your concerns. Ideally, we'd all take advantage of the insights our parents, in-laws, and siblings could offer us, without being too sensitive to implied criticisms or different outlooks. But regardless of how we interact with family, our friends help us navigate the waters of motherhood. In this chapter, we turn our attention to the people *outside* our families—to the friendships we desperately need, and that we must tend and nourish so they keep thriving.

At all stages of your life, you develop relationships with people who reflect your values and interests, or who challenge you to think outside the box. Most often, you simply like friends who make you laugh. When you become a mother, you need the buddies who'll help you in a pinch with pickups, the confidante with whom you can share your most shameful fears, and friends who are similar to you and those who are polar opposites. Even if—or perhaps especially if—you work outside the home and

FROM PROBLEM TO SOLUTION

Amy, Mother of Three from Connecticut

Too often, one child or another is upset about something when Amy leaves her house to head to work, whether it was the homework her son didn't get done, a shirt her daughter wanted to wear that was in the laundry, or the baby who was crying about the sitter. All the way to work, her kids are on her mind, and she starts her day feeling unsettled. But when she gets to the office, she grabs a coffee and heads to her friend Sarah's cubicle. Even though they both have so much to do, taking a moment to chat helps them get on with their day better. Amy unloads about her mornings, and Sarah usually offers some funny story about her own children. "I feel such a sense of relief knowing my kids are normal," Amy said, "and that every mother has the same experiences that I do!"

sometimes feel out of the loop, you crave a sense of connection with other women. Tracy, mother of two from Louisiana, said one of the biggest surprises of motherhood was the safety net and camaraderie her friends give her. "They remind me that I'm not alone," she said, "and that's been huge for me."

It's not just about our inner circle, though. The power and connection we feel when reaching out to those *outside* that cozy group—to individuals, organizations, or big-picture causes— is also vital to our overall well-being. Remembering that our everyday concerns pale in comparison to the needs of others can sometimes be what makes the difference between a positive outlook on life and an unhappiness borne of loneliness or stress. Giving back to the larger world out there will help frenzied, modern mothers put their lives—their hopes and dreams—into perspective.

> *If you want others to be happy, practice compassion. If you want to be happy, practice compassion.*
> —Dalai Lama, Tibetan Buddhist leader

The Steady March of Time

Women make their closest friends at different times of their lives. Many women have the old buddy who knows them better than anyone—the friend who remembers them as they were in the old days, before they had kids or mortgages and life got complicated. These friendships revolve around *them*, not the kids, and are like a lovely breath of fresh air.

If you're a new mother muddling through the early years of parenthood, you probably feel pretty overwhelmed. For many women, there's a lot of loneliness and insecurity. Whether you end up staying at home or pursuing a career, those years when everything feels untested and overwhelming can really leave you dying for a soul mate—someone other than your equally exhausted husband. Some of women's richest friendships are formed right when a new mother can barely finish a sentence, with one child dangling on one hip and another screaming at her side. It's in this struggle of parenting that you show the world your true self and discover the inner workings of your friends. In the process of forming these friendships, a deep trust and mutual understanding is in the making.

Charlotte, mother of five from Michigan, remembered her early parenting days as intensely isolating. She used to go to the mall, push the stroller, and hope against hope that someone would strike up a conversation with her. Mothers who go back to work have it hard, too. Janet, mother of two boys from Maryland, found it hard to connect socially with anyone outside the office because the demands at work and at home left little time for making new friendships. On the weekend at the playground with her kids, she felt excluded from the mom circle, all of whom already seemed so comfortable with each other.

> *My father always used to say that when you die, if you've got five real friends, then you've had a great life.*
> —Lee Iacocca, industrialist

Finding other sympathetic women to spend time with helps us feel less like the novices we really are. Many mothers told us they had to learn to be less passive—making the cold call to the woman they just met on the street corner, reaching out to someone they'd never met before, striking up that conversation with a stranger—even when they felt self-conscious or tired.

FROM PROBLEM TO SOLUTION

Melinda, Mother of Three from Illinois

Melinda had two middle schoolers and a toddler, *and* was new in town. "Talk about isolation! I'd see moms at playgrounds, coffee shops, ballet classes, and so on, and I'd always want to join in on their conversations," she said. Then she met a "PF"—a *potential friend* called Mary, who had two girls. They arranged a play date with the children, but it was disastrous: her older kids were difficult and her little one screamed the whole time. Melinda left feeling resentful that she hadn't had the chance to develop any kind of bond. When she got home, the phone rang and it was Mary wondering if she wanted to meet her at the park that weekend. They ended up having a great time, and the kids had fun too. "When we're just ourselves," Melinda said, "those connections will happen in spite of other circumstances."

Further along on the mothering journey, you find yourself surrounded by other parents—especially mothers—at school functions, sports events, and birthday parties. You develop many happenstance friendships. There's often a honeymoon period where you'll see mothers like you everywhere, and you feel part of a great, powerful sorority. Then, in our focus group discussions and in our own lives, we've noticed a shift in the friendship dynamic as the kids get older. Competition and jealousy often enter the picture. Everyone has a lot more going on and a lot less time, so mothers can fall into friendships that are easy and avoid ones that are time-consuming. Sometimes there's less deep or honest conversation among mothers, and they don't always know who to turn to or who to trust.

The Friendship Dance

Good friends usually know intuitively when they're asking too much of you and when they can lean extra heavily on your shoulder. Old friends have been around for long enough to know when it's time to listen and when it's time to talk. But with the new friends we make, the rules can seem obscure.

Women we talked with identified the following as the most important unwritten rules of friendships between mothers:

▶ **Do what you can.** Although it's important to reciprocate as much as you can, it doesn't have to be tit for tat.

▶ **Listen and talk.** Take the time to really *hear* what someone is saying.

▶ **Humility's the way to go.** Occasionally admitting to vulnerabilities in yourself and your family is a must.

▶ **Hospitality is key.** Make sure to open your home to kids and friends from time to time. Most people love to be invited over, and they don't care if the house is spotless or if you've cooked a gourmet meal. Burgers on the grill, a big pot of pasta, or a quick salad will more than fit the bill. It's the camaraderie in a comfortable setting that counts.

▶ **Be proactive.** Don't wait till a friend needs you to be there for them. Call, write, or say hi often.

▶ **Air grievances face-to-face.** Being forthright helps avoid resentments—if you're having problems with someone, it's best to deal with them gently but directly. When chatting with other friends, always bear in mind that it's kind to keep complaints about others to yourself.

We heard from many working mothers who felt as though they'd somehow been left out of a secret, whereas the stay-at-home moms seemed so comfortable and familiar with one another. True enough, without the flexibility in the working woman's schedule, it may be harder to have a fulfilling private life—but this doesn't mean it's impossible. When you make it a priority and open yourself up to different opportunities, you'll find new friends coming out of the woodwork.

> *Keep away from people who try to belittle your ambitions.*
> *Small people always do that, but the really great*
> *make you feel that you, too, can become great.*
> —Mark Twain, writer

Focus on Friends Who Fill You Up

From personal experience and countless stories, we learned that many mothers unwittingly get caught in friendships that drain them: the overbearing buddy whose child is a "genius," the friend who is perpetually in crisis but never actually listens to

ANNE JIGGERS THE SCORE CARD

A colleague asked one day how my kids participate in activities or play dates when I'm at work. I explained that when I can't find a babysitter, I rely a lot on friends, neighbors, and family, and she asked, slightly amazed, "Don't you ever feel guilty that friends are helping *you* more than you can help *them*?"

When I first went back to work, my kids were already involved in all sorts of activities, from Girl Scouts, to swimming, to gymnastics. I didn't want them to stop doing the things they loved just because I was working again. I cobbled together solutions one day at a time, and that left me asking quite a few favors of friends and neighbors.

But here's the problem: I was so conscious of not wanting to take advantage, that on days off and weekends I was *constantly* taking kids to fun-filled places to compensate the mothers who'd been helping me out. Then on top of that, I found myself desperately trying to pay back all the favors by having kids at my house nonstop. It left our family without a minute to ourselves.

Something had to change. I started seeking out activities for our kids that were scheduled on the days or evenings when I was home. I switched my daughter's swim team because the practice times worked better with my schedule. That enabled me to do more than my share of the driving and give my friends a break from time to time. It felt so great to be able to say, "Don't worry, I'll drive both ways to the practice," or "I'm happy to take them all to the meet on Saturday." Demonstrating a consciousness to those who have helped me is a great way to show them my appreciation.

I also decided that I needed to be really up-front about my situation. There have been days when the kids have wanted to participate in activities but I knew I wouldn't be able to do any driving around at all. It's my responsibility to have an honest discussion and explain my work schedule to my carpool friends. If they're willing to do most of the driving, I'll allow that to happen—and I'm all the more appreciative for the help! Often I'll give them a little gift of some note cards, flowers, or some home-baked cookies to say an extra thanks.

Ultimately, it's the friends with whom there's mutual trust and understanding that I rely on the most—the friends who I know are not keeping a scorecard, yet who understand that what goes around comes around.

your advice, or the old soul mate who can't stop sharing negative assumptions about you or your kids even when she hasn't seen you in years. Given the energy expended each and every day to keep ourselves and our home lives running smoothly, it's important that mothers steer clear of those friendships that *drain* rather than *give* in return.

We've all experienced the negative energy that comes from an unhealthy friendship. This is a friend who makes you feel rotten. Whether it's on purpose or by accident isn't an issue: these friends are usually oblivious to the impression they're making on you. Sometimes we carry these friends over from childhood; we're so steeped in the roles we've played for so long that we may not even notice the pattern till it's firmly entrenched. Other times it's an affable acquaintance who we may discover is doing us more harm than good.

Most often, we don't realize that these friends are affecting our stress level until it's already cranked up high. It takes some chutzpah to confront a friend like this—to "break up" with them—but when they just take, take, take, sometimes it's in our best interests to move on.

> It is one of the most beautiful compensations of this life that no man can sincerely try to help another without helping himself.
> —Ralph Waldo Emerson, writer

We all have different types of friends for different needs. Isabella from Australia has an old friend who has read every self-help book out there. Her friend is always willing to listen and give advice about Isabella's three kids without being a know-it-all. But sometimes you want someone who's been through the same things you've experienced, especially if it's serious grief, illness,

FROM PROBLEM TO SOLUTION

Sue, Mother of Two from Massachusetts

Sue really liked her daughter's friend's mother, Anna. They didn't socialize much, but talked—on the phone or when passing—about their children and various issues about how their girls were growing up. "I trusted her," Sue explained, "and I went to her a lot for advice." So when her daughter needed coaching in math, Sue asked Anna for recommendations on a tutor—but she unexpectedly got the cold shoulder. As it turns out, Anna was using a math tutor and didn't want anyone else to poach him. "I'd thought we were friends," Sue said. "But I realized she saw me as a competitor. I decided that's just not the kind of friend I need."

or dealing with a lifelong disability. Incredibly close relationships can develop between people who meet through support groups, in the hospital, or in the most unexpected places such as a specialty food store or a therapist's office. And sometimes it's just your regular community who comes to your rescue.

Farther Down the Road

Different stages of life offer us different opportunities for finding friends. Most mothers we talked with agreed that as their kids entered school, they gravitated more to "friends of convenience:" people they met through kid-related activities. If your

SUSAN FINDS SHE'S NOT ALONE

One sunny day in May, I was hanging out in my driveway enjoying all the children's activities. The air was warm, the sun was blazing, and the neighbors, young and old, had gathered to play. The kids were reveling in a "no-schedule" afternoon. I looked around and enjoyed the sight: one child roller-blading, one biking, one scootering, and one performing cartwheels with friends on the lawn. My friend Laurie had just pulled in to drop off my daughter Cole from gymnastics, and as usual drop-offs go, we heard the call, "Everyone out!" All the kids started running around and playing without a care in the world. What a nice time for parents to catch up too!

We were admiring Laurie's newborn's gorgeous blue eyes, when all of a sudden we heard a big crash and a screeching, heart-stopping scream. It was my son Carl; he'd fallen off his scooter. He came racing around the corner of our driveway, and with about fifteen people gathered now, he looked up at us with blood all over his face.

I raced to him and held him in my arms. I felt dazed, mostly because of the blood—and this was my baby! Laurie went to her car and gathered her first aid kit, while my neighbor, Mary, calmly helped me figure out what to do. I could barely think straight.

As the blood was still gushing and I was holding this terrified child, I noticed that people were just stepping in and getting things done. Laurie had brought out antiseptic, bandages, swabs—you would have thought she was pre-med! Mary had connected with my sitter and was figuring out who needed to go where. She took my other kids inside the house, called my husband to clue him in, and then decided she'd take Carl and me to the emergency room. The biggest panic turned into a well-orchestrated series of things-to-do-next. And after a couple of minutes, my heart started to beat a little bit slower and Carl's fears had died down.

That day made me realize that during almost every difficulty I've faced, it's been my support network that has stepped right in. Thank goodness for great friends and community.

son plays basketball or your daughter is a soccer fanatic, you're likely to get to know other parents from standing on the sidelines. These serendipitous friendships can save your life when you're in a pinch. Though you may not know them all that well, you often trust these people implicitly; their children bond with yours and you're likely to see them a lot more regularly than your own best friends.

*Each friend represents a world in us, a world possibly
not born until they arrive, and it is only by this meeting
that a new world is born.*

—Anaïs Nin, writer

The friends we make in this stage of life can really teach us a thing or two. When you're younger, you gravitate toward a certain type of person, and you'll often make assumptions about others based on what they look like or what they like to do. But once you become a mother, you're thrown into situations with other moms and those stereotypes go right out the window. Debbie from Texas, mother of two, tended to hang out with the nerdy types in school. She thinks of herself as a type A. Then she started working with another mother on a school committee who was a poet and a songwriter—the artistic, scatterbrained type. Unexpectedly, they got on like a house on fire. Many women talked about how much they learned from becoming friends with women whose children are older. Jean, mother of three from Illinois, said, "I really seek out the older moms. They help me keep things in perspective and stop sweating the small things!"

Mothers can learn so much from friends who do things differently. Brigit, who lives in England and has three kids, makes a point of seeking out women friends who share her values but have dissimilar personalities or parenting styles. She's convinced that hearing from voices that challenge her assumptions about how to do things makes her a stronger mother.

FROM PROBLEM TO SOLUTION

Julia, Mother of Two from California

Julia likes to travel, watch movies, and sketch in her journal. But between her job as a teacher and raising her kids, she rarely made time for any of that. Her circle of friends shrank to the parents she met through her kids' school. When she thought about the people she talked to regularly, she realized they were all carbon copies of her: suburban mothers with identical values and similar experiences. So she joined a drawing class that meets in the neighboring town. It's a mixture of men and women, single, married, young, old, with and without kids. "It's changed my life," she says. "I'm not kidding. It's great for me to really be able to discover myself again through these new friends."

> *If you want understanding, try giving some.*
> —Malcolm Forbes, financier

There's great comfort in finding common ground with people. Scientists have proven that social ties reduce the risk of disease by lowering blood pressure, heart rates and cholesterol. The director of the Center for Cognitive and Social Neuroscience at the University of Chicago, John T. Cacioppo says close relationships can have a profound effect on our cardiovascular and neuroendocrine activity: in other words, a friend's nurturing love will lower your blood pressure! So every now and then, ask yourself: Have I connected with someone new recently? Are my friends filling me up, or should I try to branch out more?

Help Yourself by Helping Others

Something that cropped up over and over again in our discussions with mothers was how we can get so wrapped up in our own lives that we forget to reach out to others who may need *us*: an acquaintance, a close-but-neglected old friend, or the larger world out there. Ironically, this unintentional closing of our minds and hearts to anyone outside our immediate, intimate circle can eventually take its toll on us by shrinking our worlds and thereby the worlds of our children, too.

It's embarrassing to admit: sometimes it takes suffering a setback to make you realize that you should be helping others—not only friends in need, but strangers, too.

As we approach middle age, it sometimes seems as though everyone around us is suffering more and more heartache, whether because of illnesses, death in the family, or divorce. When a friend of Katrin's unexpectedly lost her mother, her friends were there for her, not only right then but also during the difficult months to come. That kind of thoughtfulness and consistency means the world to someone whose unhappiness can make her feel intensely isolated. Caroline, a mother of two from Georgia, told us about her friend Jane's depression, which

FROM PROBLEM TO SOLUTION

Marlene, Mother of Four from Arizona

Marlene had friends in her neighborhood, friends from work, old school friends, and her husband's friends. In fact, she had so many friends she didn't *want* any new ones. Then she hurt her back after falling during a hike and was laid up for an entire month. To her amazement, the person who helped her the most was a shy, stiff-seeming woman whom Marlene had barely paid any attention to at all: a widow with a teenager who had recently moved onto her street. She organized a food drive, car pool, and after-school activities for Marlene's four kids. "It touched me," she explained, "because I thought I was so generous, but this woman—who'd really gone outside her comfort zone—taught me that I wasn't really practicing what I preach!"

had been getting worse and worse. Even her husband was powerless to help her snap out of it. It took a group of women and their loving intervention to help convince Jane to see a therapist and to consider taking medication. Friends in need are friends indeed.

People like to think of themselves as generous, compassionate, and nurturing—it makes them feel good. Even if your underlying reasons for being altruistic turn out to be *selfish*, the effects are still hugely beneficial. Studies have shown that acts of altruism work wonders in boosting your sense of control and satisfaction. Dr. Martin Seligman, director of the University of Pennsylvania's Positive Psychology Center, explains in his book *Authentic Happiness* that the following comprise the main elements of happiness:

- ▶ **Pleasure:** laughing, having fun, physical enjoyment in something like sex or exercise
- ▶ **Engagement:** the *depth* of our involvement in family, work, romance, or our hobbies
- ▶ **Meaning:** when we use personal strengths to serve a larger end

Surprisingly, he discovered that pleasure is *not* the greatest source of happiness for an individual. "Americans build their lives around the pursuit of pleasure," Dr. Seligman writes. "It turns out engagement and meaning are much more important."

How great does it feel to do something kind for an elderly neighbor or get involved in a charity full of energetic, hopeful young people? And we're not talking baking cookies for the school's bake sale—we mean business here: reaching out *beyond* our normal circle.

Think about when you're really down in the dumps: everything is hard, and yet everyone *else's* life seems more exciting—

or at the very least, less demanding than yours. Then think about how you feel when you do something that makes someone *else* feel great: you feel generous and competent, as though your actions have meaning and impact. In addition, a sense of connection to others is established, which can be very powerful. After all, you reap what you sow, and the world will treat you with reciprocal kindness. A 2005 University of California at Riverside study showed that five kind acts a week significantly boosted participants' happiness, especially if those five acts were committed on the same day. This proves that we can influence the level of our happiness and satisfaction by intentionally directing our energies to charitable activities.

Happiness comes from giving, not getting. If we try to bring happiness to others, we cannot stop it from coming to us also. To get joy, we must give it, and to keep joy, we must scatter it.
—John Templeton, businessman

There's a catch, though. What if you just don't have time, and this lingers on your to-do list as yet another thing that you just can't seem to wrap your arms around? Is it possible to shake yourself out of this stasis and do just *one* little thing to give back?

We establish many positive relationships for our children through the healthy, loving connections we make with the world around us. We not only model what it means to be a

KATRIN TAKES SOME BABY STEPS

Right after my kids were born, I started feeling the powerful urge to give back to the world. I was so blessed to have my healthy children, my incredible husband, and my tight-knit family and community. Suddenly everywhere I turned, I was aware of those less fortunate. The single moms, how can they do it all? Prisoners who made terrible mistakes and need *hope*. Soldiers, sacrificing themselves in our name. Women suffering violence. Not a day goes by that I don't feel the injustice of my good fortune in the face of so much suffering.

So where was I to go with these new feelings of gratitude and debt?

Umm . . . nowhere.

It was all I could do to get my kids through the day, to pay attention to my relationship with Kevin, to keep the house running, and to work on my art and writing. For the past two decades my brother dedicated his life to raising awareness about energy consumption, and I couldn't even get my act together to buy those low-energy lightbulbs. How sad is that?

Then my kids reached school age. While I still didn't have time to save the world, I did feel capable of taking one small step in the right direction. So I joined their school's active community outreach program. I felt better, but I still wasn't doing enough.

As my oldest child neared double-digits, I finally understood that all my procrastinating was leading to something unforgivable: my own children would grow up to be self-centered and spoiled. That could not happen. Guilt-ridden lethargy was not going to be my legacy!

For me it's all about taking one step at a time now. What do I really care about? *Learning: the power of words and knowledge.* What do I want to teach my kids? *That they can make a difference.* So we set up a system where some of their pocket money goes into a fund that they use to buy supplies for schoolchildren in Iraq. We stand together in the store and figure out just how many dollars can buy how many erasers, pencils, books, and rulers. The very same package of supplies my kids hold in their hands, filled with everyday things they take for granted, will be held by a child in Iraq.

It's not much, but some effort—along with the intention to eventually do more and more—is better than thinking about it and doing a whole lot of nothing.

good friend, but we give the kids the gift of close relationships with people other than ourselves. Our children develop a special sense of community and will always know there are other people out there looking out for them.

> *We make a living by what we get, but we make a life*
> *by what we give.*
> —Winston Churchill, former British prime minister

Isn't that what helps us mothers through the hard times —knowing we're never alone and that we can make a real difference?

TIPS FROM THE TRENCHES

► **Thank a mentor.** Who has had a major influence on your life? Perhaps it was your fifth-grade teacher, your old professor from college, or a distant cousin. Sit down for a few minutes, and think about what that person taught you. Write him or her a letter, or better still, make a date to meet for lunch or coffee. Share with that mentor the wonderful things he or she taught you, and say, "Thank you!"

► **Check in with your outer circle.** Every now and then, think about those people you like or admire who navigate the outer circles of your social life. Have you checked in with them at all? One of them is going through hard times—give her a call. Someone who has been lonely in the past? See if she's found her way. Another lost a parent—send her a little something to tell her you're thinking of her. Letting someone know that you care goes a long way toward making the world seem kinder and more hospitable.

► **Commit a random act of kindness.** Instead of walking past that street person, like you usually do, give him or her ten dollars. Spend a Saturday serving food with your children at a local homeless shelter. Take toys to a hospital waiting room. Have your kids take flowers to an elderly neighbor. Make a list of all the things—whether small or large—that you and your kids could do to help someone in need. You don't have to commit to months of work—just one day at a time. Be spontaneous: when you're bored, do a good deed instead of watching TV or going shopping!

▶ **Rid yourself of stereotypes.** Maybe there's a new mother in your neighborhood you don't know well but have always thought looks a little odd. Perhaps there's a new student in your child's class whose parents don't know anyone. At the sidelines of a hockey game, soccer field, or basketball court is there a parent who always seems to be on his or her own? Make an effort to invite them into your circle. Not jumping to conclusions about someone is a gift to them and to yourself.

▶ **Do something unexpected for a friend.** Is there one friend you rely on more than others? Make sure she knows how much you value her presence in your life. Create a collage of pictures of the two of you together, take her out for a meal, send her a cute card in the mail, or throw her a little surprise party with a few of her close friends.

▶ **Chuck your emotional baggage.** Take stock of a friend who leaves you feeling empty rather than filled up, and create some distance. Take back control. Figure out the minimum you need to do to keep the relationship steady, and don't give more than you get. For instance, you don't always need to pick up the phone or return a call. You can politely decline invitations or make yourself busy with other activities.

▸ **Be quick to forgive.** Maybe you have a friend who has been absentminded recently or left you out? Maybe she said something mean and hurt your feelings. Think of all the times in the past that friends have been there for you when it counted, and be quick to forgive small slights. If roles were reversed, you, too, would be grateful to be given the benefit of the doubt.

▸ **The power of the human touch.** E-mail is an incredible way to stay in touch with far-flung friends. It's easy to get in the e-mail habit with closer buddies, too, and many women come to rely on it almost exclusively. But talking in real time and hearing the tone of a friend's voice leaves you with a whole different feeling of intimacy. If you find yourself feeling out of touch or disconnected, try picking up the phone or scheduling a get-together. It may make you feel more "filled up" by your friendships.

▸ **Get a girls' night on your calendar.** Some do book groups, some do movie nights—and we've even heard of the MSMs (known to their kids as the Main Street Moms and between themselves as Moms Seeking Alcohol!). Whatever outing suits your fancy, there's nothing more fun than getting out of the house and connecting with your girlfriends. It gives you something to look forward to in the middle of a busy week and a way to connect with your buddies without the rest of your clan around.

▶ **Open up your home to others, often.** It's easy to forget to pick up the phone and invite people over, but everyone loves to get out of their own four walls. Since we can't always pull off the glorious dinner party we'd love to throw, we often simply don't have people over at all. How about setting up a weekly card game and making it bring-your-own-bottle? Or watching a favorite show with your girlfriends, snacking on a potluck dinner? Sharing a good laugh with some friends in a relaxed setting is a great way to give and get some love.

I TRIED THE TIPS! SALLY, MOTHER OF FOUR FROM MASSACHUSETTS

"I have this old friend who lives close by, who visits and calls a lot. After she goes, I'm always left feeling cranky—and I *always* feel guilty about it. I try, but I can't seem to give her what she needs from me. It really wears me out. So I tried not always returning her calls, and I let myself get really busy with my job so she doesn't come around as much. You know, excuses here and there. It didn't solve the problem completely, but it did help bring more positive energy into my life."

7

THE SIGNIFICANCE OF SELF-CARE

From Never Putting Yourself First to Taking Care of Your Whole Self

By now, it may well seem a truism that you have to take good care of yourself to take good care of others. But when in our outreach we posed the question, "Do you care for your health as thoroughly as you care for your kids' health?" not a *single mother* answered yes!

Let's face the truth: unless you're as healthy as you can be on the inside and the outside, you'll end up worse for wear—and so will your family. It's all about the big picture; you want not only to be a loving, effective mother, but also to be energetic, even-keeled and upbeat, right? Time-outs to take care of your health are a must.

The reluctance to focus on self-care is totally understandable. It's probably way down on your list of priorities. After all, who wants to get their teeth drilled? You'd much rather finish a spreadsheet or clean the bathroom than get a Pap smear or a mammogram. And who wants to spend money on a babysitter so you can get prodded and poked, or sit and talk to a therapist while the minutes tick away—minutes when you could be doing something else productive, something that *counts*?

> *Happiness is nothing more than good health and a bad memory.*
> —Albert Schweitzer, scientist

Frankly, when you're young, there's simply not that much upkeep. Then the babies come, and it seems as if you're at the ob-gyn's office every other day. During those child-bearing years, you know exactly what your blood pressure is or whether your nutrition is adequate, and scores of professionals are at hand to help you in a heartbeat if you're having concerns of any sort. Whether or not this constant upkeep is a hassle, you do it all for the health of your baby.

Then the years go by, and you begin noticing small things. Maybe you get tired more easily or don't heal as quickly. Friends and family suffer illnesses, and suddenly you know ten women with breast cancer. Premenopause hits. You start dealing with aging parents. You no longer feel invincible.

Yet aging definitely doesn't have to be misery and gloom.

Every woman can age gracefully and live a long, energetic life as long as she remembers to treat herself with care and respect. Since no one else is looking out for us the way we look out for our children, we have to step up to the plate and look after ourselves. Simply put, it's our responsibility. Kayte, mother of two from Maryland, said, "I don't put myself to bed if I feel rotten. No one's going to fluff my pillow for me." Let's change that, starting now.

The spiritual eyesight improves as the physical eyesight declines.
—Plato, Greek philosopher

No empty promises will work. To be the best mothers and women we can be, we have to put our own physical and mental well-being way up there on our list of priorities. Self-care is not just another series of mindless chores, but will bring us—and by extension our loved ones—tangible benefits.

From Not Enough Hours in the Day to Making It Happen

Studies have shown that when pressed for time women compromise on diet, exercise, and sleep. "Foregoing healthy lifestyle habits in favor of more time during the day is not the solution," says Dr. Kathryn Lee, professor in the Department of Family Health Care and Nursing at the University of California in San Francisco, in a 2007 National Sleep Foundation survey. "In fact, it can be detrimental to optimum health and performance." Peggy from Massachusetts, mother of three grown children, admitted that when her kids were little she never, ever went to the doctor. "Just think how much time I've saved not going to appointments!" she said.

Not all of us can count on having such great genes and good luck. Do you think it's worth taking a risk?

So how do women compensate for the stresses of everyday life? Certainly not by exercising: according to a 2005 survey by the U.S. Department of Health and Human Services, 66 percent of women say they *never* engage in vigorous, physical leisure-time activities for more than ten minutes a week. That's per week, not per day! Instead, they're reaching for quick fixes like caffeine, alcohol, antianxiety medications, and sleep aids. Food can become a big crutch, too.

But boy can that backfire! The more caffeine you drink, the more wired you are and the less rested you feel. That extra glass or two of wine at night that helps you unwind also makes you tired the next day. Taking medicine for your mental health issues is often a godsend to the time-strapped mother, but this can also mask deeper, underlying problems that may be better addressed by regular counseling.

There's just no way around it: we need to take our self-care seriously, and this means focusing on three main areas:

1. **Everyday self-care:** grooming, nutrition, and exercise
2. **Periodic self-care:** annual health checkups and routine tests
3. **Holistic self-care:** mental health, medical specialists, and alternative therapies

The real sin against life is to abuse and destroy beauty, even one's own—even more, one's own, for that has been put in our care and we are responsible for its well-being.
—Katherine Anne Porter, writer

OK, true enough, it may well seem that if you were to do everything necessary to care for your own health, it would be a full-time job, on top of all your other jobs. But with some imaginative thinking and lots of planning ahead, it *is* possible to methodically check off that list and ensure you don't suffer pain or anxiety unnecessarily. Here are some quick, logistical fixes we heard about that will help you get to those long overdue appointments:

- ▸ Ask a friend or a neighborhood teenager to watch your child for an hour or two so you can get a checkup.
- ▸ Every time you schedule an appointment for your child, think about your own health: do you need to consult someone about that sore shoulder, the pulsing in your leg, or the frequent headaches? Make that your *very next* phone call.
- ▸ Ask if your doctor has evening hours; many do.
- ▸ Schedule your appointment at the end of the workday, and meet your husband at the doctor's office so you can go out together afterward.
- ▸ Bring your child(ren)—and a book or drawing supplies—to the doctor's office with you.

Most important of all, remind yourself often that your family needs you to be healthy in mind and body, so taking care of yourself is simply nonnegotiable!

Those Oh-So-Elusive Z's

Remember when your babies were born and you dragged yourself through the day on a few interrupted hours of sleep? You managed because you knew—or hoped!—it would be short-lived and anyway, you had no choice. Now your kids are older, and maybe it's your job, hobby, responsibilities, or schedule that is keeping you up at night. For many women, getting enough z's ends up being a problem that plagues them long after their kids are soundly sleeping through the night.

According to the National Institute of Neurological Disorders and Stroke, the amount of sleep women need can vary widely, depending on many factors, including age. But "getting too little sleep creates a 'sleep debt,' which is much like being overdrawn at the bank. Eventually, your body will demand that the debt be repaid." As we age and our responsibilities and worries grow, we crave sleep even more; yet we're still not getting enough.

A 2007 poll by the National Sleep Foundation said that 60 percent of American women reported that they get a "good night's sleep" only a few nights a week. Whether you're a mother working outside the home or staying at home, the poll shows that your sleep problems are pretty similar. Even

FROM PROBLEM TO SOLUTION

Julieta, Mother of Four from New York

Most of us are pretty in tune with how much sleep we need on a daily basis to fully recharge our batteries. Julieta bargains with the alarm clock every morning for that extra five minutes. "I really need my sleep to be human," she said. She operated for years on only five hours a night until she realized it was one of the main reasons she was so crabby around her kids all the time. Now she goes to bed as early as 8:30éÈ Èmost nights. "Some things have to slide, like the dishes or talking with my husband, because without enough sleep I just can't make it all happen!"

though almost two-thirds of stay-at-home mothers said they spend more than eight hours a night in bed, almost 75 percent of them said they suffer from symptoms of insomnia two to three nights each week. That's a significant majority. And although full-time working mothers generally get less than six hours a night in bed, they report similar difficulties as the stay-at-home mothers concerning sleeping through the night and feeling refreshed.

Now get this: part-time working moms get the best sleep of all; a full 50 percent say they're in bed eight or more hours a night and most of them report getting uninterrupted, refreshing sleep. So what's *their* secret? Could it be that the right combination of work and time at home leads those part-timers to place themselves higher on their list of priorities?

That's a choice: you can do it too!

> There is only one thing people like that is good for them;
> a good night's sleep.
> —Edgar Watson Howe, writer

But what if you get to bed when you need to, only to discover you have trouble getting to sleep or staying asleep? Before reaching for those sleep medications, try a few of these simple solutions:

- ► Use earplugs, available at any pharmacy, and a silky eye mask. Dim all lights, shut the blinds, and turn off any electronic devices that hum or blink.
- ► Try not to engage in any vigorous activity, like working out, right before bedtime. What makes you calm before you sleep? Watching television in bed? Reading?
- ► Play a CD of gentle, instrumental music, or nature sounds, like running water.
- ► Experiment with your caffeine tolerance. Could you be drinking caffeine too late in the day? Remember, it's often a hidden ingredient in things like sodas, teas, and chocolate.

- ▶ Trade favors with your husband or your kids, and sleep in late one weekend morning; that will go toward repaying your sleep debt. But keep in mind that experts also say that if you try to go to bed and get up at around the same time *every day*, you have a better chance of falling asleep easily.
- ▶ If you wake up in the middle of the night, give in to the urge to get up. Get yourself something warm to drink—without caffeine—and then sit down for ten minutes and write a list of what's on your mind. You may find that writing things down helps stop them from racing around in your head.

Stress and the Mind-Body Connection

We shouldn't underestimate the impact that constant, unabated stress can have on a mother's health and well-being. When you're ignoring your need for rest and relaxation, not getting enough sleep, or not finding a healthy outlet for your energy, stress can build and build until you explode. Everyone has had those moments: either you lose your cool at work or home, or you absorb the stress into your body and it makes you ill. Did you know that stress can cause ulcers, jaw pain, high blood pressure, headaches, skin and weight problems, depression, and edginess, among countless other equally unpleasant things? No thanks!

According to the Massachusetts General Hospital guidelines, stress warning signals fall into six basic categories:

- **Physical:** sleep trouble, headaches, ringing in ears, back pain
- **Behavioral:** critical attitude, grinding teeth, overuse of alcohol, cigarettes, or food
- **Emotional:** crying, boredom, sense of pressure, anger, loneliness
- **Cognitive:** lack of creativity, memory loss, inability to make decisions, loss of sense of humor
- **Spiritual:** doubt, inability to forgive, martyrdom, apathy
- **Relational:** isolation, resentment, clamming up, lowered sex drive

If you notice any of these symptoms persisting, it's important to try to tackle the root cause. You may need to consider making some bigger changes to your life. Sandy, mother of two teenagers from Florida, told us she experienced many of these symptoms for years—finally developing migraines—before realizing that ignoring them wasn't helping. And what was the core problem? Part of it was her environment: Sandy hated the loud street she lived on. It took real courage for her to admit this and say, "I want to move."

There is more hunger for love and appreciation in this world than for bread.
—Mother Teresa, missionary

FROM PROBLEM TO SOLUTION

Marybeth, Mother of Three from Wisconsin

One night, Marybeth was bathing two of her kids when her oldest walked in and started bothering them. Soon there was chaos all around. "When I get tired, I yell," she said, "and I hate myself for it, but I can't stop." So she let loose. Then she caught sight of herself in the mirror. "Who is that crazy woman? I thought to myself. I was horrified by what I'd turned into." When stress accumulates and she doesn't find an outlet for it, she ends up taking it out on her kids. But when she goes for regular walks, takes ballet lessons, or dances at home with her kids, she's a completely new woman. Between jobs as an actress, she does her best to fit something active into her life so she can avoid becoming that screaming woman in the mirror.

What if the cause of stress is simply life itself? Don't despair! There are lots of manageable steps you can take, starting right now, that will get you going in the right direction. Some proven antistressors include:

- Exercising vigorously (until you break a sweat)
- Getting enough sleep—for most women, at least seven hours a night

- Having periodic quiet time: no noise, no media, no talking, just silence
- Sharing problems with friends, your husband, partner, or a professional
- Eating healthfully
- Having sex

Your Day-to-Day Look

If you're a stay-at-home mom, you've probably noticed the phenomenon of exhausted-looking mothers wearing sweats and sneakers all day long. What's the point of getting a pretty haircut, putting on makeup, or dressing nicely? When you spend the whole day running after kids and cleaning up the disaster zone of your home, it's easy to forget that looks matter.

Are we just being superficial here? No! Let's face it, it's hard for us to feel powerful, attractive, and in control if we look like slobs. One working mom from Italy, Marietta, said the best thing about going back to her job after having her third child was dressing up and styling her hair again every day. She hadn't realized just how insignificant she'd felt those years when she hadn't bothered with how she looked.

Listen to your body's wisdom, which expresses itself through the signals of comfort and discomfort. When choosing a certain behavior, ask your body, "How do you feel about this?"
—Deepak Chopra, writer

Here are three tried and tested—but super simple—fixer-uppers that mothers shared with us that actually make a difference to their day-to-day lives:

- Women who dress in "real" clothes everyday feel better. Childish, oversized clothing or stretchy exercise gear just doesn't say "respect" the way a nicely cut pair of jeans and a pressed T-shirt do.
- Those ladies with colored or highlighted hair make sure to keep up with their roots and always try to maintain their haircut. Studies show that the very first thing most people notice about others is their hair.
- Making a little extra effort by putting on some makeup, donning a pretty pair of earrings, or wearing something on their feet other than granny shoes—even when they won't be seeing anyone "important"—makes moms feel a lot more human.

You Are What You Eat

How great do you feel after you've finished off that fried chicken or a yummy, salty bag of chips (full of those evil trans fats)? As good as it tastes while you're indulging, foods that are high in saturated and trans fats, salt, and sugar will make you feel lethargic and bloated afterward—not to mention guilty.

We all know that women's relationship with food can be complicated—the three of us are living testaments to that.

SUSAN'S DIET OBSESSION

When I open up my wallet and reach way back in the dark crevasses to get stamps or some obscure business card that I've kept, I often get a quick glance of my Weight Watchers Lifetime membership card, dated 1988. Wow—nutrition has been on my mind for a long time!

After college, I worked hard to keep my weight under control. I tried fad diets, quick fixes, and "wonder" bars that were supposed to take off the weight as you were eating them. At the supermarket, anything labeled "diet" made its way into my shopping cart. By day I drank a lot of coffee, and at night I dipped broccoli into mustard for dinner. I worked late, slept little, and ran pretty hard for many years.

By my midthirties, I was feeling sluggish during the day and my sleep was often interrupted. By the time our fourth child was born (and I had gained and lost fifty pounds four times), I decided I needed to take stock of how my food habits were affecting my whole self. During my pregnancies I got used to indulging in my cravings, and I knew I needed to stop the frenzy—eating large turkey subs with bacon, avocado, and extra mayo was just not going to cut it in the long run, not to mention that I was fed up with always feeling tired.

The first step I took was gathering information about nutrition. I did lots of research online, in magazines, and in books and asked my doctor for a referral to a nutritionist (my insurance paid). Then I focused on my reactions to food. I learned that for me, it's not about the scale, it's about how food makes me feel. If I have too much rich food one night, like creamy sauces on fish or a decadent chocolate mousse, I'll suffer the next day. Now I can recognize my body's signals: if I crave protein, I eat a piece of grilled chicken or tuna; if I need sugar, I'll grab an apple. I try to buy fresh, local produce and have found that being prepared and having what I call a "happy fridge" brings me closer to my goal of healthy living.

Instead of going to Weight Watchers, every Friday I put my kids on the bus and meet my neighbor for a weigh-in, and more important, a quick "How's it going?" Having someone to talk to regularly about our nutrition goals helps keep us on our toes and connected to our whole selves.

Once women have children, they often find their bodies react differently to food. Their metabolism can slow down; they can feel hungrier or more lethargic.

Just as with so many female friendships, the bond between the three of us was cemented partly because of our many discussions about weight: before babies, after babies, and everywhere

FROM PROBLEM TO SOLUTION

Teresa, Mother of Three from Massachusetts

Teresa was in the habit of weighing herself every morning. If her weight was up a pound, she'd spend the day grumpy. Up two or three, and she'd be inconsolable. Down a few, and everything was right with the world. "It was like living permanently on a roller coaster, and I ended up getting dizzy!" she said. When she went back to work, she had less time to think about eating or weighing herself, and she started blowing off her daily weigh-in. "I used the are-my-clothes-tight-or-loose test and actually, I felt way better," she explained. "No more obsessing."

in between! Each of us has a weight range we're comfortable with, and truthfully, we often struggle to stay there or to *get* there. We know all too well that women can easily become obsessed with the pounds on the scale—whether it's one pound, ten, or twenty. Here's what we can tell you from our own experiences: it's not worth all the agony worrying about the details. Whatever the numbers on your scale or your body mass index (BMI), what really counts is that you feel strong, full of energy, and confident. The bottom line is, you'll usually feel most energetic and positive when you're not carrying around a lot of extra weight.

You'll find many comprehensive resources out there telling you how to develop healthy eating habits. Through personal experience and from the many women we talked with, we learned these bare-bones tips about a more measured way to approach our daily interaction with food:

- Only eat when you're hungry, and stop as soon as you feel satisfied. Sounds simple enough, doesn't it? If you can get your body used to listening to what it's telling you, you'll never have to diet again.
- Make a point to enjoy what you eat, and make it count by sitting down and using proper utensils.
- No food is off limits. That's right! Eat what you love, just not a lot of it. It's all about portion control: one fist is the size of *one portion,* and we're not talking the Incredible Hulk's fist here.
- Eat a small portion of complex carbohydrates (e.g., brown rice) and protein (e.g., chicken, fish, or beans), and lots of vegetables with each main meal. Fruit is good, too.
- Sorry, but alcohol has lots of calories and makes you nibble on unhealthy foods like chips and dip (it also makes you hungrier the next day). So you could try adhering to the *rule of one*: once a week, or one drink per party!
- Try to cut down on sugar and salt, using herbs for flavor instead. Remember that eating is highly habitual:

over time you might come to appreciate simpler, less
heavily flavored food.

► Learn to scrupulously read the list of ingredients
  in everything you buy. Low-calorie foods can be
  deceptively high in sugar, which creates cravings. Avoid
  too much salt, sugar (including the ubiquitous high-
  fructose corn syrup), preservatives, and trans fats or
  saturated fats.

► Try to eat foods that are as close to their natural state
  as possible: whole grain breads, not white; organic
  chicken breast, not marinated and prepackaged; home-
  made meals rather than fast food; and fresh vegetables,
  not canned. Anything white or colorless, such as rice,
  bread, and pasta, is usually not so healthy.

The American Heart Association encourages taking
omega-3 fatty acid or fish oil supplements on a daily basis (fats
from nuts, fish, and natural oils such as olive oil are healthy),
but foregoing all other vitamins in favor of getting the right
nutrients through your food. They also urge caution with using
herbal supplements: just because they're called "natural" doesn't
mean they're safe. It's probably a good idea to ask your doctor's
advice about what you might need.

*Life expectancy would grow by leaps and bounds if green
vegetables smelled as good as bacon.*
—Doug Larson, British Olympic medalist

Shake Your Groove Thing, Yeah, Yeah!

Of course, exercise isn't only about looking good, but also about *feeling* good. For many of us, exercise can make the difference between being a grumpy caretaker and a patient one. For some this means running marathons, and for others it means taking the stairs at work; everyone has their own level of ability and need.

Working out has so many benefits: it counteracts the unhealthy buildup of body fat and dissipates nervous energy that can lead to stress. According to a 1999 *New England Journal of Medicine* study, those who walk five or more hours a week (at three to four miles per hour) cut their risk of heart attack in half, and walking briskly for thirty minutes a day decreases your risk by a third. And get this: exercise can also cure insomnia, which is both a symptom of stress and a stressor.

Women we spoke with identified the following four things as key motivators to keep them exercising:

▶ **Understanding the benefits.** The payback in terms of health is huge, directly affecting the quality of your life by improving it.

▶ **Regularity.** Can you commit to regular physical activity three to four times a week? We all know that building exercise into your schedule increases your chances of seeing it through, whereas doing it when the mood grabs you makes laziness an easy way out.

▶ **Personal satisfaction.** Strenuous exercise increases your sense of satisfaction. Many women said exercising gave them a

FROM PROBLEM TO SOLUTION

Yvonne, Mother of One from Virginia

Yvonne used to hate working out, but then her doctor became concerned about her high cholesterol and weight gain, and ordered her to get moving. She was stumped. Going to the gym seemed like Chinese water torture. Weights, ugh. Spin classes? Deadly. A friend suggested she join a local women's soccer team, and so she started playing every week. Now she says getting out her aggression on the soccer field not only makes her feel strong and healthy, but it also helps her maintain her equilibrium. "Instead of bugging out, I can be home and be calm," she said. And she's made some new friends, to boot.

boost because it made them feel they had achieved something worthwhile. And being more toned wasn't so bad either!

▶ **Trying something new.** Everyone agreed they get bored with the same old patterns. Miranda from New York, mother of twins, switched from pounding the pavement to swimming at the YMCA and rediscovered her enthusiasm for physical challenges.

> *Nothing makes a woman more beautiful*
> *than the belief she is beautiful.*
> —Sophia Loren, actress

Ideally, every woman approaching middle age would concentrate on both cardiovascular activity, like running or aerobics (something that gets your heart pumping and makes you sweat) and resistance training (lifting weights). This will keep your heart healthy, your stamina high, and improve your muscle tone. Weight training has the added benefit of being good for your bones—great for women at risk of suffering from osteoporosis.

Medical Must-Dos

We'll bet you don't even think twice about taking your children for their annual checkups, and it should be the same for you. As you age, there are certain health concerns that you have to take more seriously, and preplanning becomes vital. The key is developing a personalized, master list of health-related doctors' visits you must make annually, and slotting them into your calendar methodically.

For preventive care, the following four checkups are mandatory, depending on a woman's age and medical and family history:

▶ **Annual doctor's visit.** According to our primary care physicians, a baseline physical should include:
- An eye exam to check for glaucoma (can be done annually by an ophthalmologist)
- Skin analysis for precancerous moles (can be done annually by a dermatologist)

- Pap test for cervical cancer screening (can be done annually by a gynecologist)
- Blood pressure check
- Urine test for diabetes
- Breast exam (a self exam should be done as often as possible at home)
- A stress echocardiogram to see how your heart is doing
- Blood work to check for liver and kidney function, and cholesterol levels

▶ **Dentist appointments.** Every six months for a cleaning and checkup

▶ **Mammogram.** Yearly after age forty (earlier if you have a history of breast cancer in the family)

▶ **Colonoscopy screening.** According to the American Cancer Society, starting at age fifty you should have a screening, unless your family has a history of colon cancer. If that is the case, you should get your first colonoscopy at age forty, or ten years before the age at which your youngest relative was diagnosed (whichever is earlier). Follow up every five to ten years, depending on your doctor's recommendation.

Consider your own family history, and consult with your doctor to make sure you don't overlook something important. Many illnesses such as cancer, eye problems, or heart disease can be avoided through diligent self-care.

FROM PROBLEM TO SOLUTION

Dawn, Mother of Two from Washington

Dawn was in her early twenties with a new baby when her father, not yet sixty years old, died of a stroke. A few years earlier, he had started taking better care of himself, giving up smoking and drinking, cutting out all sugar from his diet, and beginning to take long walks to strengthen his heart. But it was too little, too late. The shock of losing her father so suddenly made Dawn take a long, hard look at her own habits. "I said to myself, I want to be there for my kids," she explained. "I realized if I didn't start *right then* thinking about the big picture of my health, I'd put everything at risk."

> *Good fortune is what happens when opportunity meets with planning.*
> —Thomas Edison, inventor

Digging Deeper

Being healthy isn't just about nutrition, exercise, and regular checkups. It's also about keeping an eye on how you're doing mentally and checking in with specialists for any more complicated issues. We tend to sweep deeper problems under the rug, hoping we'll just get over them, but there comes a point when this just isn't tenable anymore.

ANNE GETS REAL

I was thirty-two years old when my twins were born, and I
definitely had more energy then than I have now, ten years
later. I thought I was invincible. An annual physical? Hmmm,
maybe, maybe not. Dentist? Not if I could avoid it. Haircut?
Only if I was really desperate. If I ever made it to any of
these appointments, it had probably taken me three tries
to get there. Something would always get in the way—a
mix-up with a babysitter, a better offer from a friend, or I'd
simply forget to look at the calendar that day.

The years passed. Gray hairs started to sprout, and
wrinkles appeared. I had a root canal here, a broken
tooth there. Allergies kicked in. Driving at night became
impossible because I couldn't see anything. Then people
around me (people my very own age) started to get sick.
One friend was diagnosed with breast cancer, another
with skin cancer, and one with thyroid problems. Ever more
frequent sleepless nights got me thinking: if I was starting to
break down on the outside, I better get to the doctor and
make sure that everything's all right on the inside.

But how in the world was I going to find time to get
there and not let the rest of life get in the way?

Last New Year's Eve I made a resolution: I was going
to start taking care of myself from the inside out. I would
make appointments, and through hell or high water I would

keep them. I told my kids and my husband what I was doing and vowed that nothing would get in the way. "If you all need to come with me, you're coming!" I insisted.

I made a list, and man, was it long. Allergist, dermatologist, eye doctor, annual physical, hairdresser, dentist, therapist, and gynecologist. I just kept plugging away at the list until I checked off all the boxes. Yes, it's a huge pain and takes lots of time and juggling to get there—but it's now midyear and I haven't missed an appointment yet!

> The measure of mental health is the disposition to find good everywhere.
> —Ralph Waldo Emerson, writer

Here's a startling piece of news: major depressive disorder is twice as likely to occur in women as in men, and 14.8 million Americans suffer from it in any given year, according to a 2003 article in the *Journal of the American Medical Association*. But depression isn't the only illness that can crop up as we age—sometimes problems we had in the past can resurface as we parent our own children. Sarah, divorced mother of one living in California, said that as her son emerged from toddlerhood, she began experiencing extreme anxiety and

FROM PROBLEM TO SOLUTION

Kelsey, Mother of Three from Maryland

Kelsey's family was having some financial problems. For months on end she'd wake up in the middle of the night, unable to get back to sleep. She tried sleeping pills, but they made her groggy the next day. She started analyzing her own emotional patterns, both in the present *and* in her past. Was it really lack of sleep or stress about money that was the problem? She decided to see her doctor and explore whether or not she might also be suffering from depression. "There was something more serious going on," she said. "Something I couldn't fix with sleeping pills." She still has her low moments, but finding a part-time job and dealing directly with her depression through mental health consultations and a mild antidepressant has helped her sleep through the night.

couldn't figure out why. It was only after seeing a therapist that she realized her relationship with a domineering father had given her deep insecurities that she was suddenly having to deal with again.

Nowadays, during routine appointments, most primary care physicians—especially the female ones—check in with their patients to see how they're managing their emotional lives: How's your family? Your job? How are you feeling? This focus on the whole self pays off by nipping problems in the bud, so you can continue to be healthy, both physically and mentally.

Juggling all the demands of life as an adult can create new psychological hurdles for mothers, and sometimes we need an extra hand in learning how to deal with them. The stigma of seeing a "shrink" is long gone; ask your doctor for a recommendation, because it might make the difference between suffering in silence and feeling confident about yourself, as well as positive about your future.

Thinking Outside the Box

Mothers are the family's unofficial first-stop doctor; according to a 2003 Kaiser Family Foundation survey, 80 percent of moms assume the primary role in choosing the family doctor and taking children to appointments. In our outreach we discovered that, for the sake of their children, mothers often think outside the box when figuring out how to cope with challenges such as autism, attention disorders, depression, and severe allergies.

Sometimes, when it comes to treating kids, the conventional route may seem too aggressive or clinical. Or maybe they've tried everything and nothing worked, but they're simply unwilling to give up. Joan is a mother from Michigan whose three kids have nasty allergies. A friend told her about Chi

KATRIN DRAGS HER HEELS

About five years ago, I decided to get in better shape.
My spirits were low, and I wasn't really looking forward to
putting on a bathing suit anytime in the next millennium.
So I started running more regularly and hitting the gym. I
worked myself really hard.

After my workouts, I'd be sitting at the computer
working and a stream of self-abuse would go through my
head: Why are you so tired? You only ran a few miles
today. Next time you have to push harder. So the next
day I would run more or faster. I'd be exhausted. I'd sit in
front of that computer and think: Wow, you better get your
act together! Maybe you're still not trying hard enough.
I frequently had to stop mid-run because I was so tired. I
started lifting weights to see if I could build up my strength,
but each day, instead of feeling better, I felt worse.

Since I have hypothyroidism (a condition for
which I have to take daily medication to regulate my
metabolism), I'm supposed to go to the endocrinologist
at least once a year and have my blood checked. I'd
skipped my September appointment, and now it was
May. Then I ran out of meds, and for a whole month I
didn't get a refill. Why? Who knows, I was too busy to
worry about it.

It was already summer when I decided I better do that blood work. The lab results came in, and my doctor called me immediately. "Can you even stand up?" she asked me.

"What do you mean? Yeah, I can stand."

"Haven't you been feeling *exhausted*?"

"Well, actually now that you mention it . . ."

Turns out I was severely anemic (there wasn't enough iron in my blood), and they couldn't figure out why. After having various tests, including a colonoscopy, I learned I'd developed something called celiac disease. This means my body can't tolerate gluten anymore, and so eating wheat was making me sick.

I felt a mixture of relief and despair at this news. No more bread, pasta, or beer—bummer. But at least I knew I wasn't to blame for what I had thought was lethargy. What a wake-up call! Until that moment, I'd never realized just how hard I am on myself.

Energy Healing sessions: "I didn't believe it could work," Joan said, "but actually, my kids can get through spring now without sneezing and wheezing! And the whole process was kind of cathartic."

How about being imaginative when it comes to considering therapies that could help you? It might be that experimenting with unconventional approaches to some typical physical and mental challenges that you face as an overworked adult is a good option—especially if you've become tired of the prescription-ready, hurry-up-and-go attitude that pervades many more traditional medical practices. Conventional Western medicine focuses mainly on solving the particular problem (through surgery or medication, for example), with less attention paid to prevention. Holistic, or alternative, healing practices look at the mind, body, and spirit of the person to identify the underlying imbalance that's causing the disease. More and more, these fundamentally different approaches to illness and healing are coming together. Get this: that traditional bastion of education, Harvard Medical School, now has a tenured professor in alternative medicine!

The doctor of the future will give no medicine, but will interest his patients in the care of the human frame, in diet, and in the cause and prevention of disease.
—Thomas Edison, inventor

Clearly, traditional and alternative medicines each have their benefits and limitations, but using both in conjunction can be the key to a healthier life. To find out more, ask for a referral from your doctor, a trusted medical practitioner, or a friend or family member. Make sure whoever you find has verifiable evidence of some success in the treatment you're considering and is willing to work with the other health care professionals in your life.

Some of the more common alternative options are:

- ► **Chiropractics:** mainly for spinal problems, but also for ear infections, migraines, and arthritis
- ► **Acupuncture:** may sound implausible but can treat anything from chronic and acute pain; to neurological, digestive, and immune disorders; to addictions and depression, anxiety, and insomnia, according to the World Health Organization
- ► **Meditation and visualization:** helps with stress management, depression, anxiety, and insomnia
- ► **Craniosacral therapy:** reduces mental stress, neck and back pain, and some chronic nervous conditions

Motherhood takes a lifetime of intense physical and mental effort. All along the way, whatever stage you're in, it's easy to put your self-care needs on hold. But in our experience, taking on the responsibility of putting yourself first, because no one else will, is what can make the difference between a balanced home life and one in which you feel put upon, unappreciated, or just plain exhausted.

Working toward the health of our bodies will nurture our inner selves, not just help us become "yummy mummies." What does this mean in practice? It means accepting ourselves, in all our imperfect glory, while pushing our bodies to function well so that we can all be healthy, active, adventure-seeking grandmothers someday.

TIPS FROM THE TRENCHES

▸ **Make a personalized master list of medical must-dos.** Take stock of the appointments you need to make, both with regular doctors and with specialists. Create a document on your computer (so you can add to it or delete as necessary) that lists them all and notes how often you're due to go. Write the phone number of each relevant doctor right there on the list. For example, if you're over forty, you'll need a mammogram each year. Type in your doctor's name and number, and the month during which you're willing to have your test *every year.*

▸ **Plug those appointments right into your calendar.** A major impediment to going to the doctor or the dentist is having to pick up the phone and make the appointment in the first place. But if it's on your calendar, you're much less likely to blow it off. So get out your master list of doctors, and sit by the phone. Call each and every one, and plug it all into your master calendar. You can always change them later if you need to, but you'll never again have an excuse to avoid getting your teeth cleaned or going for follow-up physical therapy. When you've done it once, it gets much easier—just make sure to always schedule your next appointment *before* leaving the doctor's office.

► **Shoot for a physical goal.** To commit to living an active lifestyle, it helps to have a clear objective, like being able to dance without running out of breath, entering a 5K race, trying to complete a triathlon, or being able to increase your weights or repetitions when doing resistance work. It's all relative: decide what's right for you and pick a goal that's achievable, but challenging. Don't make the goal about your weight—make it about a physical achievement that you'll be psyched to work toward.

► **Focus on the froufrou.** What gives you that extra little jump in your step? Maybe it's when you've recently had your hair done or when your skin is smooth and soft. Take the time to treat yourself each and every week to one beauty routine that makes you feel great: rub scented lotion on your neck and shoulders, wax your legs (at home or professionally), or paint the nails on your hands or feet with a cheerful color. It doesn't take a lot of money to hone in on the details, just a little time and effort.

► **Skin care is paramount.** Women who look and feel beautiful often have "glowing" skin. This is mostly due to great skin-care routines that keep their faces clean and moisturized. Make taking care of your face a priority: exfoliate two or three times a week, use an SPF cream every day, slather on lotion after a shower, and always take off your makeup at night. Every drugstore now sells inexpensive facial products that can make the difference between looking tired and feeling fresh.

▶ **Be mindful in the supermarket.** When you're grocery shopping, don't forget about *you*! Put the foods you like and need on the weekly list, not just what others in your household want. Then you can make yourself a fresh, filling salad (with some protein from chicken or tuna, and some good fat from olive oil or nuts) instead of nibbling on the children's artery-clogging chicken nuggets.

▶ **Compensate for crashing early.** Many mothers crawl into bed at an ungodly early hour (if they can pull it off) because they know they need sleep. Who suffers? The spouse! That time at night when the kids are in bed or quietly doing their homework is usually when couples reconnect. If you need those hours to catch up on z's, make sure to find an alternative time to connect with your partner: maybe an early morning walk before the kids are up, a regular lunch date, or the occasional night away together.

▶ **Keep track of your menstrual cycle.** Many women find their moods and bodies change at that time of the month. Use your everyday pocket calendar to scribble small notes about your cycle. Make a special note when you notice yourself becoming more irritable than normal, when you're more hungry or not as hungry, and most important, when you're fatigued. It's even helpful to jot down when you have a headache, jaw pain, or perhaps back pain: all of these are signs of hormonal changes in your body and can also be caused by stress. This way you can become more aware of your "typical symptoms," preparing for them before they blindside you.

▶ **Glug, glug, glug that H$_2$O.** Drinking lots of water is crucial to our well-being: we should all be drinking at least eight glasses of pure water a day. Water has no chemicals, additives, or calories and has countless health benefits: it removes toxins and waste products from our bodies, keeps skin hydrated and glowing, aids with weight loss, reduces headaches, and helps with digestion!

▶ **Track food mood.** Everyone's been lectured endlessly about keeping a food journal, but this is different. To figure out what the best diet is for us as individuals, we need to know how food makes us *feel*. When you drink too much alcohol, that hangover you get the next day lets you know you over-indulged. But what about when you eat a lot of bread or red meat or sweets? Do you notice a change in how you feel the next day? Experiment with eliminating one or two items from your repertoire, and see if you notice a positive change in your energy level.

You are the only person alive who has sole custody of your life. Your particular life. Your entire life . . . not just the life of your mind, but the life of your heart. Not just your bank account, but your soul.

—Anna Quindlen, writer

I TRIED THE TIPS! CASEY, MOTHER OF TWO FROM CONNECTICUT

"I used to be in really good shape, but then I just got busy and lazy, I guess. When I started huffing and puffing just climbing a couple of stairs, I knew it was time to do something. I tried your suggestion about setting a goal for myself, and I thought, what can I handle? What would be hard but also fun? So I decided to sign up for a race. I started running one mile on a treadmill every other day. At first I ran a thirteen-minute mile! Every week I upped the ante a bit, until just last month I was up to five miles, at ten minutes a mile. Now I've signed up for my first 5K race, and I tell you, it feels great!"

8

THE POWER OF LESS

From Living a Frenzied Life to Gaining Greater Control

Almost any mother you talk to will say that what she craves most is a sense of control. Women's lives get so cluttered with activities and possessions that sorting through and organizing it all can give them a real headache. The funny thing is that although the mothers we talked with felt they're doing more, earning more, and having lots more stuff, they're enjoying it all *less*.

But it's not like that for everyone. We also heard from women who've begun the journey of gaining more control over their busy lives by paring down their acquisitions and activities. It frees them up in so many ways: they have more space to breathe and think; there's less anxiety about buying, upgrading, and organizing; and best of all, they have more peace of mind (not to mention more actual time) to spend doing the activities they love with their families.

Many mothers admit to feeling as though they're drowning in stuff, and although most prefer their weekends to be less crammed with activities, they find themselves succumbing to the pressure to constantly be on the go. Remember the good old days when you were a kid and would play outside on a tire swing for hours on end, or save all your change for that one record you couldn't live without? That appealing simplicity often seems to be what's missing from our busy modern lives.

Just the fact that you're a parent means you'll accumulate stuff whether you want to or not. As our kids get older, they outgrow everything. Their activities become more and more complicated, they start playing multiple sports, and they need new books and better equipment. Before you know it, you're surrounded by shoes, jackets, arts and crafts supplies, jump ropes, scooters, rusty bikes, and helmets. Sharon, mother of three from Massachusetts, said her husband is the culprit in her house: he's such a "gear head," she can barely make it through her hallway because of all the sneakers, fishing supplies, wet suits, tennis rackets, and balls lying around.

On top of what you amass through the simple process of living, as you enter middle age you often start inheriting family heirlooms such as furniture, books, and pictures. It never seems to stop! Did you know that self-storage facilities in the United States have increased by 36 percent since 2001? According to a 2007 *New York Times* article, there's enough self-storage space to cover three times the size of Manhattan. Why is this industry one of the fastest growing in America? Because we have so much stuff that we can't cram it all into our homes.

> Waste is worse than loss. The time is coming when every person who lays claim to ability will keep the question of waste before him constantly.
> —Thomas A. Edison, inventor

But waste is the new pariah. At this pivotal moment in history, as our mass culture begins embracing a more measured, forward-thinking approach to the world and its resources, mothers are starting to feel the power. They can make the choice to embrace a simpler, less materialistic approach to life and really feel good about it. From recycling, to reusing, to simply not indulging in excesses, many mothers we spoke to felt energized and committed to making changes that would positively impact their future and the future of their families.

Less is truly more. When so many overwhelmed mothers crave simplicity above all else, how is it they get so caught up in endless clutter and complications? Is it possible for us all to be happy with less? Couldn't we all say, enough already?

Being Open to the Unexpected

We've talked at length about simplifying our own agendas so that we, as women, can make our own needs more of a priority by taking some time-outs for ourselves. But when our family calendar is filled with the inevitable play dates, school events, sports games, away tournaments, and enrichment activities (not to mention appointments to fix Tracy's braces, get little Sean's eyes checked, or take Violet to her tutor), how do we make time for our families to breathe?

> *Making the simple complicated is commonplace; making the complicated simple . . . that's creativity.*
> —Charles Mingus, musician

The vast majority of the mothers we talked to in Europe as well as in the United States felt the pressure—from society *and* from their kids—to constantly be on the go. A clear indication of America's competitive drive to achieve is its attitude to youth athletics. A 2005 *New York Times* article said that twenty-five years ago only 10 percent of kids treated by Dr. Lyle Micheli, director of sports medicine at Children's Hospital in Boston, had injuries from overuse, but that number had risen to 70 percent. It all starts innocently enough, taking your four-year-old to a neighborhood soccer game. But before you know it, she's on the traveling team and you're spending hours in the car. In addition, other activities and hobbies are plugged in—they're seen as necessary enrichment so your child is well-rounded—and hey, presto, you've got total mayhem!

In fact, many mothers are so accustomed to being constantly occupied that free time becomes something they actu-

FROM PROBLEM TO SOLUTION

Tory, Mother of Two from California

Tory's kids were almost teenagers when she realized her family schedule had gotten out of control. She barely saw her husband anymore because they were each so busy taking a child here and there, or getting this and that—she couldn't even remember the last time they'd all hung out together as a family playing a board game or talking over a long dinner. "One day, I just realized I missed them all," she said. Tory decided to take control of her schedule and make choices about what to cut out. "I became ruthless about turning things down," she explained, "because I understood that I was the captain of this ship, and if I wanted peace, I was the one to make it happen."

ally avoid. Julie, a mother of one grown child from Maryland, told us about her cousin who works full-time and just can't sit still. Even the kids always have something to do or something electronic in their hands to keep them busy. "They're always so strung out, never able to relax," Julie said.

It takes time to be imaginative, to ponder the world and yourself, and to feel truly present in your life. Making space for that time is a gift to yourself *and* your family. Susan from New Jersey, mother of two, said she starts her workweek in a better

ANNE TONES IT DOWN

By nature I'm a doer—life is too exciting not to experience it all. Having identical twins, I wanted nothing more than for them to have the opportunity to differentiate, and so I let them try lots of things to see what would be a really good match for their personalities. Living by this philosophy created a super busy schedule, especially once my son Jay came along! There were new activities, new faces, and new things for my kids to try. But don't get me wrong—I loved our adventures.

We seem to have done it all: play practice, swim team, karate, after-school ballet, soccer, lacrosse, hockey, and art class. But here's the rub—I also like to engage fully in whatever I'm doing. So I'm always late. It not only bothers me, as I frantically try to make up for lost time, but it starts to bother everyone else, including my kids!

I can't count how many times I've been headed somewhere like a soccer practice or a lacrosse game and a friend happens to be driving by and stops to say a quick hello. Before I know it, I have five minutes to get to a field that's twelve minutes away. I push it another minute or two—I'm having fun, and I'm genuinely interested!—but I still end up having to cut off the conversation abruptly.

Pulling out of my driveway, I'm frustrated. My son or daughter asks what time we're supposed to be at the field, and I answer with my standard phrase, "We're not late

yet!" (knowing darn well that we've only got two minutes
to get there). Inevitably, I peel into the parking lot a full ten
minutes late. My heart is pounding, I'm sweating, and the
kids are mad.

It's taken me many years to realize that if I don't clear
the decks a bit to seize the moments when they present
themselves, then I'm really missing out on life. I decided I
needed chunks of time to let the day unfold, so I have time
to finish a phone conversation with a close friend or take
five minutes with a neighbor. I've become much choosier
in what we do and have learned to say no—not an easy
task for me. It's allowed me to take the extra few minutes
with the teacher at school or to nurture the child with the
skinned knee. It's simple, really: I'd rather be calm than
frantic.

frame of mind if she's had the weekend to decompress with her
family. "The weekend, for me, is *not* the time to get stuff done,"
she said, "it's time to be together as a family."

If your child falls off his scooter and has to get an x-ray,
do you need to make ten calls to cancel activities for the day?
What if it's a Saturday afternoon and your seven-year-old sug-
gests selling raffle tickets together, going to the corner store
for fun, or doing an art project—is that serendipity something

your schedule can accommodate? Half the fun of life is being open to the possibilities that present themselves out of the blue. You never know what fun might be lurking right around the corner, if you only had a little more leeway to accommodate the unexpected!

Clearly, people have totally different attitudes to free time. Type A mothers like to be busy; type B moms prefer a slower pace. What we've discovered is that even if you're a gung-ho doer with an action-packed schedule that keeps you content, eventually you'll reach a tipping point.

> *True affluence is not needing anything.*
> —Gary Snyder, poet

Sometimes it's about finding and establishing a rhythm that fits your style rather than allowing your schedule to overwhelm you. Ultimately, it's about being proactive rather than reactive. If you're dying for an afternoon at the museum with your middle child, then cancel the tutor, postpone the community meeting, or say no to painting the scenery for the class play.

The entries on your calendar represent choices you make about what you want to do and when. Try giving something up to get something back.

The Avalanche of Acquisition

Most of us eventually realize that having a lot of stuff doesn't necessarily bring happiness (even if the shopping part can be fun). Dawn, mother of two from Oregon, said, "If I never got one more thing in my life, we could live the rest of our lives and be just fine." Many women get to the point where possessions begin to feel burdensome: they need to be managed, and they're distracting. The women we spoke to who lived in small spaces often claimed a wonderful sense of freedom from the impulse to buy—they simply don't have the storage capacity and that kills the desire to shop.

Enough is a feast.
—Buddhist proverb

Let's stop for a moment to think about the effect that filling our lives up with things and activities has on our children. Madeline Levin, author of *The Price of Privilege,* says that when kids are overscheduled, they "can't find the time, both literal and psychological, to linger in internal exploration, a necessary precursor to a well-developed sense of self." So many mothers in our outreach complained about the agony of managing their kids' voracious desire for more, new, better stuff. Our consumer culture has so profoundly influenced our notion of mothering that we fret about depriving our little girl of her very own princess bedroom or fancy party dress, or letting our son be the only one in his class without his own cell phone, even if we can't easily afford these items. Not to mention how worried we get about whether our kids really need the latest computer program that will help them excel in school, or their own personal lap-

SUSAN DISCOVERS HER INNER ARTIST

All it takes is for October to roll around, and my heart starts racing. In our family, three of our six birthdays and four of the seven major holidays all happen within two months. I used to dread this time of year. I'd panic about kids' party invites, Halloween candy, goodie bags, turkey brining, goodie bags, Christmas presents, goodie bags, and so on.

Inevitably, come mid-December, I'd be frantically searching for that perfect painted dinosaur set or that midsize telescope with all the features for night viewing. Since I have four kids, I always tried to keep the total number of presents reasonable and even, but my buying frenzy was getting out of control.

Last year I decided to keep my evenings free so I could quietly do needlepoint for an hour or so. I'd been working on a sports pillow for my son Hugh since the previous January, and I figured I might be able to finish it for him someday before he went off to college!

The quiet time gave me a chance to still my mind, to be creative and work toward a goal. As November rolled around, I realized I could possibly finish this project by Christmas. I worked slowly and enjoyed every minute of it. After all, if I was doing needlepoint, by definition I was relaxing.

On Christmas day, we all opened wonderful stockings from Santa, shared great stories over a special breakfast with my parents, and then it was time to get to the big stuff. I glanced over and saw Hugh holding this mushy, rectangular package, and I knew it was the moment of truth. After tearing off the wrapping paper, he reached over to give me the largest unsolicited hug he'd ever given me. Since he's not a big, proactive hugger, this was a really precious moment. Sure, he loved the other "big" items he got, but it was the pillow that brought him the most joy. He sleeps with it every night without fail.

Isn't it funny—the simplest activity brought us both the greatest joy. And in a neat twist, what settled me down is exactly what settles him down every night.

top, or that really expensive but "guaranteed to promote learning" game from Zany Brainy or The Right Start.

It's no surprise that the educational toy market is the fastest-growing sector of the industry: according to a 2007 *Harvard Business School Bulletin*, a company called Leap Frog that makes electronic reading devices became popular so fast that it became the third-biggest toy manufacturer in the United States after only seven years. It's hard to say no to something when you think it may give your kid an edge!

Where do you stand on this issue? How do you feel when you hash out with your family what they need and want—do you find it overwhelming? Do you often give in, even when your gut says it's excessive?

> *Always bear this in mind, that very little indeed is necessary for living a happy life.*
> —Marcus Aurelius, Roman emperor

You may find that the less you fill up your life with possessions and activities, the more you can develop and enjoy an inner life. For children and adults alike, when you have the mental space, you can do the following:

- Enjoy solitude and peace.
- Find your own happiness.
- Get pleasure from reflective thinking and being creative.
- Enjoy spontaneity.
- Continue to forge ahead after experiencing disappointment or failure.
- Understand the value of moderation, hard work, delayed gratification, and compassion.

The bottom line is that everyone wants to feel loved for who they are inside, not for what they have. Every human being craves a genuine connection with the world, and that con-

FROM PROBLEM TO SOLUTION

Helen, Mother of Three from Delaware

Helen's family loves gadgets. They have the latest in everything, from video gaming devices and computers, to cell phones and cameras. On Helen's birthday a few years ago, they were all out for a nice family dinner, but she was distracted by the goings-on at the neighboring table: two teenagers were playing on their Game Boys throughout the entire meal, while the parents sat side by side silently. "I felt so bad for them," Helen said. "It was as if they were all just sitting there completely *alone*." That image stuck with her, and she decided to pare down on the time her family spent on media. "I met with so much resistance, but I didn't give in. We like each other's company, so why not actually pay attention to each other?"

nection can't develop if it's not given some space and time to blossom.

Here are some things to think about as you contemplate buying more items for yourself, your home, or your children:

► Do you already have something else that might work just as well? If you think you need another end table, can you refinish a neglected table instead of buying a new one? Why not frame a beautiful painting your child made, rather than buying something new? As we embrace a leaner culture in which waste is no longer tolerated, recycling and reusing will become the norm.

▶ When buying gifts for friends, family, or kids, really focus on what would be lasting and useful, rather than something that gives temporary pleasure but soon becomes junk. Does your buddy really need another set of napkins or a vase, or would a book be more thought-provoking?

▶ For every item of clothing you buy for yourself or your children, give one item away. This will remind you of how much you already have, and how much others may benefit from what you routinely discard.

▶ Could you save the money that you might otherwise spend on little extras—another pair of shoes, nicer sheets, more knickknacks for your children—toward something that will create lasting memories, like a weekend away with your family?

> *From contentment comes supreme happiness.*
> —Maharishi Patanjali, Hindu philosopher

Less Is More: Living It

If we stop for a moment, and take stock of what drains us in our daily lives, we can make the conscious choice to rid ourselves of the excess. Here, being selfish means determining your own standards—what you feel comfortable with—and then sticking to your guns.

Many families feel compelled to buy things even when they can't really afford them. In his book *The Pursuit of Happi-*

ness, David G. Myers talks about how feeling happy is relative to our prior experiences. "If our current condition—income, grade-point average or social prestige, for example—increases, we feel an initial surge of pleasure," he explains. "We then adapt to this new level . . . come to consider it as normal, and require something even better to give us another surge of happiness."

FROM PROBLEM TO SOLUTION

Julie, Mother of Two from Massachusetts

Julie and her husband, Toby, worked in the financial industry for fifteen years before they had kids. They'd already put aside a little nest egg when Julie quit work to focus on her children, one of whom has severe language processing delays. "Before kids, we used to go out a lot for fancy dinners, to the opera, and all that jazz, and I had a beautiful outfit for each occasion," she said. But slowly, dealing with a developmentally challenged child made Julie and Toby begin to alter their lifestyle. Where they had previously found such joy in lots of action and glamour, they started to prefer hanging out at home, rather than dressing up and going out on the town. "I care much more about simple things, the little joys and achievements," she said. "Funny enough, we really don't get the same satisfaction anymore from the things we accumulated in all those years as big spenders."

In other words, it's a natural tendency for humans to always want more, even when they know better. Caroline, mother of three, grew up in rural North Carolina. "Back home, people had no college fund," she said, "but they'd always have the latest stereo!" Once she became an adult and had her own family, she began to understand that, "a healthy soul is the key to success, not being perfect or having everything you want."

> *A peaceful mind is your most precious capital.*
> —Swami Sivananda, monk

There's no doubt about it, beautiful objects can fill us up with joy. Almost every woman gets some satisfaction from treating herself to something pretty every now and then, buying her children the perfect gift, or finding just the right item to make her home especially cozy. No one we spoke to suggested embracing a vow of poverty, but almost universally, mothers said their lives felt more balanced when they were surrounded by less stuff.

What's Your Comfort Level?

We all have and require possessions, and we've got to figure out how to manage them. This is such a personal thing: some mothers can't be happy unless their houses are spotless, while others are fine with a bit of a mess. One thing is for sure, even if you tidy up constantly, your house won't stay that way. Within

FROM PROBLEM TO SOLUTION

Ruth, Mother of Two from Pennsylvania

Whenever Ruth went to her friends' houses, her heart would sink. How do they keep their homes so neat, she'd ask herself, when my place is such a dump? It weighed on her so heavily that she started avoiding visiting them. If it bothered her that much, she wondered, why wasn't she doing something about it? Working full-time and hating housework, she didn't feel she could handle the problem without more help than her husband or kids could offer. She decided that a cleaner house was more important to her than getting take-out food every other night, so she hired someone to come in and help tidy up once a week. "It's still not perfect, but I realized I didn't need perfect," she explained. "I just need *less mess.*"

half an hour of clearing out your hallway, one of your children will have tracked in dirt, dropped a toy, or thrown a jacket onto the floor. That's called living.

Can one compare any joy to that of taking things quietly, patiently and easily? All other joys come from outward sources, but this happiness is one's own property.
—Hazrat Inayat Khan, Sufi teacher

Do mothers *really* have the time and inclination to label drawers and separate their children's clothes by color? Some do, but we discovered that in most cases, the honest answer is no. Moreover, trying to attain and maintain this level of organization sucks up all your spare time and can become an obsession. These moms are trying so hard, yet they feel like failures over and over again.

The key is to identify what drains us personally and to prioritize those areas. To feel at peace, Connie and her husband, Jerry, who live in Utah, need to have a clean house, cleared of clutter. To not drive themselves nuts, they enlist the help of their three children, who all have regular chores to do, and Jerry spends one morning each weekend just tidying up the garage. To them, the effort is worth it.

What you consider clutter depends on you as an individual, but when objects are neither functional nor appreciated, are crammed into spaces that are too small, or are so disordered that you can't find them when you need them, then they are clutter. Make up your own mind how you feel about it, and if it bothers you, get rid of it!

Managing the Mess

Let's say, like most mothers, you'd prefer your home to be reasonably well organized. We have heard countless little tricks that women use on a daily basis to give themselves a sense of calm in the chaos of motherhood:

- They lay out their clothes and the kids' clothes the night before.
- They put the kids to bed in clean clothes that they can wear the next day. (Yes, it works like a dream!)
- They make the kids' lunches and have them pack their school bags before heading for bed.
- They leave the kitchen clean so that when they wake up in the morning, they're happy to get up and make breakfast.
- They set the coffee machine on automatic so they wake up to the aroma of fresh-brewed java.
- They teach the children to make their own breakfast and to put away the dishes.
- They check their daily calendar *before* going to bed, so they know what's in store for them the following day.
- They keep the kids' schoolwork or "treasures" in individual plastic buckets that they sort through at the end of each school year.
- They take the mail out of its envelopes and throw away all junk and advertising *as soon as it arrives.*
- They have one designated area in the kitchen for papers, another for invitations, and another for notices to act upon.
- They delete or file e-mails *once a day.*
- They act on every phone message as soon as they listen to it.

KATRIN MAKES PEACE WITH DUMPSTER DIVING

When I met Kevin, I was a slob. My room in the basement flat I shared with my best friends was a window into my soul: posters taped up onto every square inch of the walls, clothes all over the floor, piles of books everywhere, and papers covering my tiny desk. We didn't own a vacuum cleaner. Kevin was delighted: finally, he'd met a girl who was his soul mate.

When we were first married, we lived in the basement of my parent's house in London. Luckily, they didn't *see* our mess much, because with all the stuff lying on the floor they could barely open the door of our room. But slowly my habits started to change. When we were graduate students, I bought our very first vacuum cleaner and hung up a few less posters on our walls. Piles got smaller. Floors got cleaner.

The thing is, Kevin didn't change with me. He was still the dumpster diver extraordinaire.

What is a dumpster diver, you might ask? It's someone who picks up "treasures" discarded by others. Those treasures might include a wooden mask, a broken wingback armchair, a full leather-bound set of Shakespeare's plays complete with etchings, a nail-care kit from 1950s Japan, a boar's head, a framed picture of a pirate, a broken rake—

these are only a few of the things Kevin has picked up in the last twenty years.

Beauty is in the eye of the beholder. Once we stopped crisscrossing the country (with endless boxes of junk in tow) and settled down, there came the issue of decorating.

"Buy stuff?" Kevin asked, incredulous. "Why buy anything? You can find all sorts of treasures and plenty of useful stuff, too, for free."

For a while it drove me crazy; I wanted some order in the chaos. Then I was hanging out with a decorator friend who was eyeing some of the stuff we have on our shelves. "My clients pay a lot for me to find these kinds of things!" she said. I had always liked the colorful, slightly thrown-together look of our home until I started to feel it just wasn't "grown-up" enough. Now I say to hell with being grown-up. At least the floor's clean.

For many mothers, acknowledging their intentions is enough to alleviate some of the pressure. Marnie from California, mother of four, likes to create long, detailed home-improvement lists. "I don't even need to achieve everything on that list," she explained, "but putting it all on paper makes me realize nothing's so terribly urgent."

It's easy to get caught up in how other mothers are running their lives—we feel envious of their homes or possessions, or jealous that they juggle everything so easily. Insecurity comes with the territory when the job is so big. Sometimes it seems as though every other mom magically gets it all done: they have their homes in order, great kids, and are happy, to boot.

> *I have no money, no resources, no hopes. I am the happiest man alive.*
> —Henry Miller, writer

Sometimes this is true, but usually it's an illusion. No one, *no one*, is perfect! It's an enormous relief to drown out those voices, to stop caring what others think, and to focus on your own personal comfort level. Once you've done that, it's all about taking action. Maybe it's your attic or basement that gives you nightmares, or the sports rack you've got crammed into the small front hallway. As with any chore, tackling it one small step at a time is what will get you closer to your goal.

> *Life is really simple, but men insist on making it complicated.*
> —Confucius, Chinese philosopher

It's also vital to work out with your kids and your spouse what your tolerance levels are. Mothers we talked to tried all sorts of things to make this tug-of-war a little easier on themselves, and these are the top four lessons they learned:

FROM PROBLEM TO SOLUTION

Chantal, Mother of Two from France

Chantal, stepmother of a teenager and mother of a middle schooler, said her big hang-up is the phone. "The constant ringing makes me batty!" she said. Even though they don't get many telemarketers calling, just the shrill ring tone breaking into her evening after she got home from work was enough to ruin her mood. Now she regularly mutes the ringer and makes sure to check for messages throughout the evening. "All my friends know to call me in the mornings if they need to reach me urgently. Not being interrupted makes the apartment seem much more peaceful to me."

► Giving up on perfection makes everything a lot easier—after all, life is a work in progress.

► Insisting that your partner does everything your way is a no-win situation. If you can give an inch, he'll give an inch too. Compromise is the only way to go.

► Pinpointing just a handful of things that really drive you crazy is crucial. Explain and *show* through your actions how happy it makes you when those things are in order. Be honest with yourself about what's bothering you: is it really that your son drops his towel on the floor, or is it maybe that you're mad about his not showing his appreciation on a daily basis?

FROM PROBLEM TO SOLUTION

Natalie, Mother of Three from Arizona

When at the baseball field watching her son's game, doing a school pickup, or attending a meeting for a parent-teacher organization at a fellow parent's house, Natalie always felt demoralized by the conversations going on around her. Everyone seemed so plugged in, so capable, and so energetic and busy. Complaining to her husband about how this running commentary on life made her feel incompetent and lazy, he simplified things for her. "He asked me, 'Is that your perception or is that reality?' I realized, I'm doing OK!" she said. "It's the second-guessing that makes me feel bad, not the fact that I'm actually doing anything wrong."

▶ Organizing and decluttering is a gift to yourself and is best when done according to *your* standards, not to impress your neighbor or mother-in-law. It's your life and your home.

Why do women like spring-cleaning (or at least, its aftermath) so much? Because clearing the dust and debris from our lives makes us feel freer and more in control. Once we've made peace with the way we manage our households—both our possessions *and* the family calendar—we can move on to the really important things in life: enjoying our surroundings;

being fully present with the people we love; doing valuable, interesting things with our time; and having some fun in between.

> The West wants the people of the poor countries to live as we do ourselves. We pity the nomad who is clearly "poverty-stricken." We fail to understand that his life can be more satisfying than our own.
> —Robert Theobald, economist

TIPS FROM THE TRENCHES

▶ **Stick to your guns.** Part of learning to be more selfish is about learning to stick up for yourself. When you've made a decision about something—"No, we won't buy you that video game," or "Yes, you have to keep up your commitment to ballet"—don't waver. Be strong in your convictions. Try being understanding, but firm: "I know you're frustrated, I've felt that way, too. But I've made up my mind, and please don't ask me again." You may have to repeat this a few times, but that's OK.

▶ **Give the gift of your time.** Consider giving the gift of time instead of something material. For kids, go on an outing, like a picnic or a trip to a museum. For an adult, why not give a bottle of wine along with an invitation to come on over and share a glass with you one night? Sure, it feels great to find a present that's perfectly suited to someone and to see joy on their face. But how often do you buy a gift out of obligation and not because it will bring real delight? Sometimes our offerings end up being burdens, whereas our time is always appreciated.

► **Clear ruthlessly.** All it takes is being regular and ruthless about sorting through what goes on behind those closed doors, and you'll feel like a million bucks. Each season, give to the Goodwill any clothes or shoes you haven't worn in the past year or two. Buy some good hangers and some nice-smelling sachets. Refold and rehang. The key is to be consistent: go through everything, including your kids' closets, at least twice a year.

► **Take a break from the supermarket.** Our pantries, kitchen shelves, and refrigerators can get so out of control: three-year-old flour, ten-year-old vanilla essence, stale crackers; globbed-up sauces; and freezer-burned chicken. Once every few months, don't go food shopping for a week or ten days. Force yourself to eat only what you have in the house. This requires real perseverance (no fresh fruit or veggies, no takeout). You'll be amazed at how much food you'll find hidden in the depths of your cupboards, and you'll finally throw away the stuff you're just never going to eat.

► **Use only *one* portable master calendar.** Having a single place in which you note down all your commitments is essential. You'd be surprised by how many women in our groups had a calendar by the phone, one in their bags, and a to-do list on their desk. Having to coordinate more than one appointment book is setting yourself up for failure. It's easier to find a midsized calendar that fits in your purse or computer bag in which you write each and every item you must do and remember. Many women like to use electronic planners, but we've met a lot who prefer the old-fashioned way. Seeing a month-at-a-time on a double page keeps them always in the know about where to go!

► **Streamline bothersome bill paying.** Except for the particularly well-organized, most mothers complained about managing the family's paperwork. Many put it off until the teetering piles become overwhelming. Signing up for an online bill-paying service through your bank can save you huge amounts of time, as can setting up autopay systems for regular, fixed expenses, such as car payments, insurance, and your mortgage. Get rid of as many paper bills as you can—the initial time invested setting it all up will save you endless hours in the long run. (Or here's a really quick fix: get your husband to do it all instead!)

► **One big file for each child.** Buy a three-inch, three-ring binder for each child. Create sections for the following: birth certificates and passports, report cards from school, written comments from teachers or specialists; copies of important e-mails or correspondence; and medical information (e.g., tests, copies of annual physicals, optician's prescriptions). File the most recent information up front. Keep extraneous or time-sensitive paperwork, such as information about seasonal camps and activities, in an open tray.

► **Experiment with delayed gratification.** The next time you need to buy something (e.g., sheets, socks, furniture, a book), put it off. Wait a day. Then wait another day. If you're really brave, wait a whole week. Often, when that week is over, you'll find you don't really need or want that object anymore. It's empowering to realize that you don't have to succumb to the urge to buy.

▶ **Analyze *why*, not just *what*.** Every time you think of something you want for yourself, your house, or the children, ask yourself these four questions:

1. Do I need it, or is it optional?
2. Can I reuse (borrow or inherit) something else instead?
3. Will it make me happy or improve the quality of my life? (Don't forget that what makes you happy in the short term might end up making you unhappy later, when you have to figure out where to put it or how to get rid of it!)
4. Can I afford it *now*? If it's a stretch, it will probably add stress to your life.

▶ **Consider being radical.** Sometimes it's refreshing to do something radical and really shake things up. If your cluttered household has been getting you down or you're drowning in bills, consider a moratorium on *all new acquisitions*. You can do it for a week, a month, or a year. There are groups throughout the United States experimenting with this minimalist approach and discovering the freedom that comes with it. It will be hard—but nothing will teach you faster about the benefits of simplicity. It brings its own amazing rewards: time, money, clarity and a whole new sense of purpose.

I TRIED THE TIPS! HENRIETTA, MOTHER OF THREE FROM TEXAS

"At first I thought your idea about not going food shopping was insane, but I figured I might as well give it a go. My pantry was stuffed to the gills with all sorts of sauces and condiments we never used, so I decided I'd finally try them all out. Well, after almost two weeks, I'd worked my way through ancient boxes of noodles and the various frozen mystery meats. I decided not to buy any more prepared foods or packaged sauces at all, and suddenly my pantry's tidy and well-stocked, not overflowing and nasty."

IT'S SUPPOSED TO BE FUN!

From Being a Good Girl to Breaking a Few Rules

Remember what a thrill it was to break the rules when you were a kid? Sometimes it was scary, but mostly it was just plain old fun. Then you grew up and started *making* the rules. All of your childhood you waited for this freedom; yet now that you have it, do you use it? Somehow making the rules took all the fun out of breaking them. It started to feel good to be virtuous, and having fun was something we did only when taking a breather from real, everyday life.

> *We should consider every day lost on which we have not danced at least once, and we should call every truth false which was not accompanied by at least one laugh.*
> —Friedrich Nietzsche, philosopher

We all know parenting is serious business. Sometimes it's hard to believe how thoughtlessly we took on this incredible responsibility, and we worry whether we can possibly do it right. Every action or inaction seems fraught with potential disaster. Maura, mother of two from New York, confessed she could hardly sleep the first few years of her daughters' lives, she was so overanxious about their safety. Steven Levitt, author of *Freakonomics*, says, "Fear is a major component of the act of parenting. No one is more susceptible to an expert's fear-mongering than a parent." So while it's OK to be vigilant and to take your job as a parent seriously, it's also important to shrug off the smaller problems, to go with the flow, and to get silly every now and then. We laughed and laughed in our focus groups at some of the stories moms told us about what "good" trouble they get into when they let their hair down.

Fun with the Kids

As adults and parents, we may feel all grown-up, but giggling uncontrollably at a youngster's inadvertently hilarious insight, rolling down a hill next to a squealing toddler, or watching your son or daughter fall in love will fill you up with the spirit of youth, winding the years right back and giving you renewed energy. When it's raining, Tricia, mother of two from California, will sometimes jump on the trampoline with her kids. Maybe it's silly and childish, but boy is it fun!

By their very presence, children give us the best gift of all —reminding us to see life through fresh, unjaundiced eyes: the

FROM PROBLEM TO SOLUTION

Sadie, Mother of Five from Massachusetts

People tease Sadie all the time about her brood, assuming that her house is run like the U.S. Marine Corps. Sure, things are hectic with lots of sports and schoolwork and the occasional night away from the kids, and Sadie can be a bit of a drill sergeant. But the best thing of all about having a big family, according to her, are their dance contests. "We whoop it up big-time," she explained, "with costumes, big hair, and glitter. Even the boys!" They blast the music, and each of them—even Ted, the two-year-old—gets five minutes in the limelight. "We always end up rolling around on the floor, laughing and being silly. It's such a great release."

weeds that they see as beautiful yellow flowers, the glow on the horizon after the torrential rain, the joy of finding a beloved old object under a bed, or a smelly, muddy dog who for them is pure magic.

> *When in doubt, make a fool of yourself. There is a microscopically thin line between being brilliantly creative and acting like the most gigantic idiot on earth.*
> *So what the hell, leap!*
> —Cynthia Heimel, writer

FROM PROBLEM TO SOLUTION

Claire, Mother of Two from California

Claire and her husband, Tony, were having a hard time once their kids hit the teenage years. The kids were checked-out most of the time, and the atmosphere at home was almost always tense. When Tony's mother gave them a nice set of bicycles for their wedding anniversary, they started taking early morning rides together. "We race each other. We made up prizes and punishments for whoever loses, always stupid stuff like someone has to give a back rub, buy flowers, or get spanked. We totally act like kids again. That makes it such a blast!"

One of the most satisfying things about being a parent is having fun with your children. Sometimes it takes looking at those cheeky little faces to remind us what having fun is. Here are a few of the silly antics mothers shared with us:

- ▶ Skinny-dipping in a neighbor's pool
- ▶ Cranking up the music in the car on the way home from a family dinner out and then dancing together in the garage
- ▶ Doing a Chinese fire drill at a stoplight: everyone jumps out, runs around the car once, and changes seats
- ▶ Playing charades with young and old

▶ Letting a child sit on the driver's lap and take the wheel
  Caution: parking lots or driveways might be a little
  safer than the highway!
▶ Going to the beach in a downpour: kick off your shoes,
  run around, and come home soaking wet
▶ Having a squirt gun or water balloon fight with a
  bunch of children
▶ Being a goofball with your kids when they've invited
  friends over—embarrass them a bit; secretly, they love it
▶ Playing hide-and-seek—and *really* hiding
▶ Having a hula hoop contest: you'll be amazed at how
  those little hips can swivel

I like work, it fascinates me. I can sit and look at it for hours.
—Jerome K. Jerome, writer

Fun with Your Man

Now what about our poor stressed-out husbands? Most of them
carry the burdens of life just as heavily as we do; they just have
a different way of expressing it. So instead of spending your free
time with your mate hashing out this month's credit card bill
or talking about your son's school report, try having a good old
laugh instead. Irene from Vermont said she feels most positive
about the future when she and her husband have tears rolling
down their eyes from laughing at something together. "Doesn't
happen often," she said, "But when it does, it's magic!" Some
silly ideas we heard:

- ▶ Riding around town on a rented scooter: let your hair down and feel the wind
- ▶ Making love in every room of the house; countertops may be hard, but fun nonetheless
- ▶ Going sightseeing on a nudist beach (you'll certainly have a giggle)
- ▶ Holding hands while screaming in terror on a roller coaster
- ▶ Dancing till the wee hours—break a real sweat
- ▶ Getting a hotel room, and *not leaving for twenty-four hours straight*
- ▶ Challenging each other to a minigolf game
- ▶ Having a picnic of baguettes and cheese by the side of a river
- ▶ Playing strip poker—and *no insecurities* (after all, no one's perfect!)
- ▶ Letting loose at an outdoor rock concert
- ▶ Being at a great party, and deciding to blow off the babysitter, breaking curfew like a bunch of teenagers

Your Own Kind of Fun

We all spend inordinate amounts of time trying to be "good girls" and do the right thing. Well, sometimes it's good to be bad. We're just human beings after all! Increasingly, parents act like they used to as teenagers, but in the inverse: hiding their vices from their kids as they did from their own parents—as though revealing one little kink in their skintight armor will cause the children to revolt. But really—as we tell our *kids* all the time—life is about moderation and knowing your limits.

> Rest and laughter are the most spiritual and subversive acts of all. Laugh, rest, slow down.
> —Anne Lamott, writer

If breaking the rules can sometimes be fun, so can simple pleasures that we overlook because we think we've outgrown them. Do any of the following things make you smile? We heard them all in our talks.

- ► Buying and *wearing* a pair of pink high heels
- ► Cranking up your favorite song on the car radio, and putting the pedal to the metal
- ► Watching one chick flick after another on TV, while drinking wine, propped up on pillows in bed
- ► Getting that favorite ice-cream dish and eating the whole thing—without guilt!
- ► Gathering your girlfriends and playing card games while drinking cocktails
- ► Having sex when the kids are downstairs
- ► Wearing that top that's a little revealing or the pretty dress that may be a bit tight—go for it!

FROM PROBLEM TO SOLUTION

Emma, Mother of Three from New Hampshire

Emma gets to sneak off with her girlfriends for a night when her husband takes the kids to see his parents. She and her buddies cram into a small motel room overlooking the sea, armed with a cooler full of goodies. Someone always comes with a huge bag of beauty supplies from the local drugstore. "We sit around talking 'til we're blue in the face, doing our nails, and slathering ourselves in lotion," Emma said. "I feel like I'm thirteen years old again, without any of the angst!"

- ▶ Treating yourself to a full body massage
- ▶ Unless you're addicted, having a single cigarette or one martini isn't going to kill ya!
- ▶ Nor is a ride on a motorbike!

Let's face it, being a martyr is no fun. We should indulge ourselves every so often, take a load off and be foolish. As long as we don't endanger our children or ourselves, we need to occasionally break free of our constraints. What you do and say shows your children how to have fun, how to love someone with passion, how to let loose sometimes, how to fight without being cruel, when to call it quits, and how to be honest.

And if we can learn not to take ourselves too seriously, to laugh with others—and sometimes at ourselves—life as a mother will be less stressful and a lot more fun.

> *Thousands of candles can be lit from a single candle, and the life of the candle will not be shortened. Happiness never decreases by being shared.*
> —the Sutta Nipata, Buddhist scripture

Mothers Need Time-Outs, Too

You want what's best for your kids, and so do we—even though we're the ones saying that being selfish isn't always bad. What we've learned over the years has changed our lives and the lives of our loved ones for the better: *being a little selfish goes a long way.*

When we are whole and happy, our children are more resourceful and appreciative, and our husbands less beleaguered. When we take time-outs, everything that seems frantic and off-kilter slips into place, and life feels a lot more balanced. Our kids notice it. Our husbands are happier. There's positive energy all around!

The end result of all these choices you can make—and the actions you'll take based on those choices—is that you can start living a more authentic life. How great does it feel to shrug off your worries about what other people think of you, your mothering, your household, and your kids? In the long run, when you're a confident and fulfilled mother, everyone's happier.

Taking responsibility for your own happiness by setting your own standards and working toward fulfilling them will help you find something in each and every day to feel grateful for. If you can find genuine happiness in the simple rhythms of life, understand and respect your needs, appreciate your loved ones, and enjoy peace in your own home, you, too, will be able to find greater joy in motherhood.

REFERENCES

CHAPTER 1: The Attitude Shift

Allen, Jon, Ph.D. "Aiming Too High May Miss the Mark." *Perspective*, no. 3 (2003) http://www.menningerclinic.com/resources/ prospective_magazine/3_2003.htm.

National Center on Drug Addiction and Substance Abuse at Columbia University. "Family Matters: Substance Abuse and the American Family, A Casa White Paper." (2005) http://www.casacolumbia. org/Absolutenm/articlefiles/380-family_matters_report.pdf.

Richardson, Cheryl. *Take Time for Your Life: A Seven-Step Program for Creating the Life You Want.* New York: Broadway Books, 1998.

University of Texas. "Perfectionism: A Double-Edged Sword." (2004) http://www.utexas.edu/student/cmhc/booklets/perfection/perfect .html.

U.S. Department of Labor, "Change in Employment by Major Occupation and Sex, 2005–06." *MLR: The Editor's Desk* http:// www.stats.bls.gov/opub/ted/2007/jun/wk2/art02.htm.

CHAPTER 2: The Power of Self-Awareness

Adams, Douglas. *The Hitchhiker's Guide to the Galaxy.* San Francisco: Del Ray, 1995.

Brenner, Helene, Dr. *I Know I'm in There Somewhere: A Woman's Guide to Finding Her Voice and Living a Life of Authenticity.* New York: Gotham Books, 2003.

Cameron, Julia. *The Artist's Way: A Spiritual Path to Higher Creativity.* New York: Tarcher, 1992.

Chopra, Deepak. *The Deeper Wound: Recovering the Soul from Fear and Suffering, 100 Days of Healing.* New York: Harmony Books, 2001.

Grupp-Phelan, J., R. C. Witaker, and A. B. Naish. "Depression in Mothers Presenting for Emergency and Primary Care: Impact on Mother's Perceptions of Caring for Their Children." *Ambulatory Pediatrics* vol. 3, no. 3 (May 2003): 142–146.

Kabat-Zinn, J., Z. Segal, J. Teasdale, and M. William. *The Mindful Way Through Depression: Freeing Yourself from Chronic Unhappiness.* New York: Guilford Press, 2007.

Kriegel, Robert. *Sacred Cows Make the Best Burgers: Developing Change-Ready People and Organizations.* New York: Warner Books, 1996.

PRNewswire, *News and Information.* "Problems at the Top—Apathy Contempt for Managers." (January 21, 2005) http://www.prnewswire.com/cgi-bin/stories.pl?ACCT=109&STORY=/www/story/01-21-2005/0002869774.

Proctor, Charlene, Dr. *Let Your Goddess Grow: 7 Spiritual Lessons on Female Power and Positive Thinking.* Birmingham: The Goddess Network Press, 2005.

CHAPTER 3: The Importance of the Here and Now

Bianchi, Suzanne M., John P. Robinson, and Melissa A. Milkie. *Changing Rhythms of American Family Life.* New York: Rose Series in Sociology, Russell Sage Foundation Publications, 2006.

Dux, Paul E., Jason Ivanoff, Christopher L. Asplund, and René Marois. "Isolation of a Central Bottleneck of Information Processing with Time Resolves fMRI," *Neuron* vol. 52 (2006): 1109–20.

Oz, Mehmet, Dr. "Here's to Your Health!" *O, The Oprah Magazine* (January 2003) 129–36.

Roberts, Donald F., Ulla G. Foehr, and Victoria Rideout. "Generation M: Media in the Lives of 8–18 year olds." The Henry J. Kaiser Family Foundation Study 7251 (2005): 9–35.

Stein, Joel, "Just Say Om." *Time* (July 27, 2003) http://www.time.com/time/magazine/article/0,9171,1005349,00.html.

Wallis, Claudia. "Are Kids Too Wired for Their Own Good?" *Time* (March 19, 2006) http://www.time.com/time/magazine/article/ 0,9171,1173991-4,00.html.

CHAPTER 4: The Value of Downtime

ABC News. "Work, Worry and Accomplishment Define Mothering in America, 2006." *Good Morning America/Good Housekeeping Poll* (2006) http://abcnews.go.com/images/Politics/1006a1 Motherhood.pdf.

Cameron, Julia. *The Artist's Way: A Spiritual Path to Higher Creativity.* New York: Tarcher, 1992.

Consumer Reports. "Sleeping Pills: Are They Worth the Risks?" (2006) http://www.consumerreports.org/cro/health-fitness/drugs -supplements/sleeping-pills-9-06/overview/0609_sleep-pills_ov .htm?resultPageIndex=1&resultIndex=1&searchTerm=September %202006%20sleeping%20pills.

National Institute of Neurological Disorders and Stroke. "Brain Basics: Understanding Sleep." (2007) http://www.ninds.nih.gov/dis orders/brain_basics/understanding_sleep.htm.

CHAPTER 5: The Loving Link with Your Partner

ABC News. "Poll: American Sex Survey, A Peek Beneath the Sheets." *Primetime Live.* (2004) http://abcnews.go.com/Primetime/Poll Vault/story?id=156921&page=1.

Blanchflower, David G., and Andrew J. Oswald. *Money, Sex and Happiness: An Empirical Study.* National Bureau of Economics Research Working Paper No. 10499 (May 2004). JEL No.I1, J3 http://www.dartmouth.edu/~blnchflr/papers/w10499.pdf.

Fields, J. "America's Families and Living Arrangements: 2003." *Current Population Reports.* U.S. Census Bureau, 2004, 7.

Gottman, Dr. John, University of Washington Department of Psychology http://www.gottman.com.

Laumann, E., A. Paik, D. Glasser, J. Kang, T. Wang, B. Levinson, E. Moreira, Jr., A. Nicolosi, and C. Gingell. "A Cross-National

Study of Subjective Sexual Well-Being Among Older Women and Men: Findings from the Global Study of Sexual Attitudes and Behaviors." *Archives of Sexual Behavior* (2006) http://www.accessmylibrary.com/coms2/summary_0286-30172387_ITM.

Newsweek Online. "No Sex Please, We're Married: Are Stress, Kids and Work Killing Romance?" (June 22, 2003) http://www.prnewswire.com/cgi-bin/micro_stories.pl?ACCT=617800&TICK=NEWS&STORY=/www/story/06-22-2003/0001969545&plain News=&EDATE=Jun+22,+2003.

Park, Alice. "Sexual Healing." *Time* (January 12, 2004) http://www.time.com/time/magazine/article/0,9171,993150,00.html.

Popenoe, D., and B. Dafoe Whitehead. "The State of Our Unions: Social Indicators of Marital Health and Well-Being." The National Marriage Project, Rutger's University (2005): 17–31.

Real, Terrence. *How Can I Get Through to You? Closing the Intimacy Gap Between Men and Women.* New York: Fireside, 2002.

Seligman, M. *Authentic Happiness: Using the New Positive Psychology to Realize Your Potential for Lasting Fulfillment.* New York: Simon and Schuster, 2002.

Weiner-Davis, Michelle. *The Sex-Starved Marriage: A Couple's Guide to Boosting Their Marriage Libido.* New York: Simon and Schuster, 2003.

CHAPTER 6: The Need to Reach Out

Cacioppo, J. T., et al. "Loneliness and Health: Potential Mechanisms." *Psychosomatic Medicine* vol. 64, issue 3 (2002): 407–17.

Seligman, M. *Authentic Happiness: Using the New Positive Psychology to Realize Your Potential for Lasting Fulfillment.* New York: Simon and Schuster, 2002.

Taylor, S., L. Klein, B. Lewis, T. Gruenewald, R. Gurung, and J. Updegraff. "Female Responses to Stress: Tend and Befriend, Not Fight or Flight," *Psychology Review* 107 (2000): 411–29.

Wallis, Claudia. "The New Science of Happiness, What Makes the Human Heart Sing?" *Time* (January 8, 2005) http://www.time .com/time/magazine/article/0,9171,1015832,00.html.

CHAPTER 7: The Significance of Self-Care

American Cancer Society, http://www.cancer.org.

American Heart Association, http://www.americanheart.org.

Kessler, R. C., et al. "The Epidemiology of Major Depressive Disorder: Results from the National Comorbidity Survey Replication." *Journal of the American Medical Association* vol. 289, no. 23 (2003): 3095–3105.

Mason, J. E., et al. "A Prospective Study of Walking as Compared with Vigorous Exercise in Prevention of Coronary Disease in Women." *New England Journal of Medicine* vol. 341 (1999): 650–58.

National Institute of Neurological Disorders and Stroke, "Brain Basics: Understanding Sleep" (2007) http://www.ninds.nih.gov/ disorders/brain_basics/understanding_sleep.htm.

National Sleep Foundation, "Stressed-Out American Women Have No Time for Sleep: Stay-at-Home Mothers Most Likely to Sleep Poorly." (2007) http://www.sleepfoundation.org/site/apps/nl/ content2.asp?c=huIXKjM0IxF&b=2434067&ct=3618771.

Pleis, J. R., and M. Lethbridge-Cejku. "Summary Health Statistics for U.S. Adults: National Health Interview Survey, 2005." *National Center for Health Statistics: Vital Health Stat* series 10, no. 232 (2006): 232.

Wyn, R., and V. Ojeda. "Women, Work and Family Health: A Balancing Act." The Henry J. Kaiser Family Foundation Issue Brief 3336 (2003).

CHAPTER 8: The Power of Less

Gannon, Suzanne. "Hooked on Storage." *New York Times* (March 8, 2007).

Levine, Madeline. *The Price of Privilege: How Parental Pressure and Material Advantage Are Creating a Generation of Disconnected and Unhappy Kids.* New York: HarperCollins, 2006.

Myers, David G. *The Pursuit of Happiness: Discovering the Pathway to Fulfillment, Well-Being, and Enduring Personal Joy.* New York: Avon Book Series, 1996.

Pennington, Bill. "Doctors See a Big Rise in Injuries as Young Athletes Train Nonstop." *New York Times* (February 22, 2005).

Young, Susan. "Toy Story: The Educational Toy Market Teaches Serious Lessons About Competition." *Harvard Business School Review*, vol. 80, no. 1 (2007).

CHAPTER 9: It's Supposed to Be Fun!

Levitt, Steven D., and Stephen J. Dubner. *Freakonomics: A Rogue Economist Explores the Hidden Side of Everything.* New York: William Morrow, 2006.

INDEX